Master Your Money Workbook

Master Your Money Workbook

Ron Blue

The 10-Week Program to
Master Your Money

THOMAS NELSON PUBLISHERS
Nashville

ISBN 0-8407-3393-3

Printed in the United States of America
1 2 3 4 5 6 — 98 97 96 95 94 93

Acknowledgments

Since *Master Your Money* was originally published in 1986, much has changed in our world. We have seen a significant stock market crash, Eastern Europe and Russia have opened up economically and politically, real estate prices throughout the country have softened, and we have begun to see the full implications of the Tax Reform Acts passed under the Reagan administration.

As I reviewed *Master Your Money* for a revised edition in 1991, I made many significant changes reflecting our changed economic environment. The sections on taxes, estate and investment planning, and insurance were changed fairly dramatically to reflect the maturing of my own thinking.

However, in working through this material again for the *Master Your Money Workbook,* I have been struck by how little has changed since 1986, relative to money management and financial planning. God's laws are timeless regardless of changing economic situations.

While adapting the principles and techniques of *Master Your Money* into a workbook format did not take as much time as the original writing, it has been a significant undertaking, one which could not have happened without the creative vision of Janet Thoma of Thomas Nelson Publishers and the collaborative efforts of Debra Klingsporn of Minneapolis, Minnesota.

However, there are many others whose influence, encouragement, and counsel have been invaluable in both my personal and professional life.

I owe a deep debt of gratitude to my parents, Don and Emma Blue, who have been a source of encouragement throughout my life.

My wife, Judy, and five children, Cynthia, Denise, Karen, Tim, and Michael, in spite of suffering through the writing of *Master Your Money,* have given me constant encouragement and joy! It is because of my wife that I came to know Jesus Christ as my personal Savior, and her unswerving godly walk for more than two decades has been a source of spiritual encouragement and challenge.

Ralph and Anne Walls of Indianapolis, Indiana, have been our spiritual parents, friends, partners, clients, and counselors throughout the last twenty years.

Howie and Jeanne Hendricks of Dallas, Texas, were the ones who initially challenged me into my current business. They are faithful and trusted advisors.

For years, two special friends, Bruce Wilkinson of Atlanta, Georgia, and Dr. Bert Harned of Mesa, Arizona, encouraged me to write *Master Your Money*.

Bruce Cook of Atlanta and Steve Douglas of San Bernardino, California, with whom I worked on the "I Found It" Campaign, provided much of the material on goal setting and faith planning found throughout the original edition of *Master Your Money*.

Larry Burkett of Dahlonega, Georgia; George and Marjean Fooshee of Wichita, Kansas; and Howard Dayton of Orlando, Florida, all wrote books on financial planning long before I did and had a major impact on my thinking as a financial planner.

Chuck and Cynthia Swindoll of Fullerton, California, graciously gave of their time and experience in helping me work through many of the difficult issues that come in tackling a project such as this.

My partners and staff were very patient with me during the original writing process, but especially Mina Breeden, my former secretary, and Regina Kreiner, who faithfully typed and edited the book, often working on short notice and with many other demands upon their time. I am indeed grateful for their work.

I especially want to thank Zoe Custer, my secretary for four-plus years, for her work in coordinating the revisions in the 1991 edition and for her efforts in contending with tight deadlines to move the *Master Your Money Workbook* toward completion; Russ Crosson, author of *Money & Your Marriage,* who contributed significantly to the estate planning section; Bob Hostetler, one of my former partners, who helped revise the tax chapter for the 1991 edition; and again the staff of Ronald Blue & Co. for their patience, support, and encouragement.

Lastly, but most important, my Lord and Savior, Jesus Christ, has again proved Himself to be faithful, and apart from Him I would have nothing to say.

Contents

PART THREE

A Forward Look

PART ONE

The Questions You're Asking

Will I Ever Have Enough?

At the age of twenty-four, I had every ingredient needed for success—an MBA degree, my CPA certification, a well-paying job with the world's largest CPA firm in their New York City office, a driving ambition to be a success, and a supportive and very intelligent wife.

For the next eight years, I put everything into succeeding at my goals and the hard work paid off. By the time I was thirty-two years old, I had achieved every financial and success goal I had set for myself:

- I had moved rapidly up the corporate ladder.
- I had founded the fastest growing CPA firm in Indiana and today it has become one of the fifty largest firms in the United States.
- I, along with others, owned two small banks in Indiana.
- I had a lovely wife and three young daughters.
- I had all the trappings of success: a new home, new cars, country club memberships, and the like.

I had also just committed my life to Jesus Christ—a commitment which began to change my perspective and my priorities.

It was during the early seventies, and for the first time in the nation's history, Americans began experiencing "tremendous" inflation rates of 4 percent and 5 percent. The prime rate hit an unbelievable high of 10 percent and then even went to 12 percent. The dollar was taken off the gold standard, and for the first time in recent history, the United States began running a trade deficit.

In the midst of personal affluence, I began to experience fear and anxiety about my family's financial future. With our country's economic climate heading for greater uncertainty I began wondering, *Will I ever have enough? If I do have enough now, will it be enough when I retire? How much is enough?* In working with people in the areas of investment management and financial planning for nearly twenty-five years, I have found few people for whom money is a neutral issue. Everyone, rich or poor, asks themselves these underlying questions—more frequently than we like to admit.

Another question, of perhaps much greater significance, confronts the Christian. Once I committed my life to Jesus Christ, I had to ask myself, *What is the appropriate lifestyle for a Christian?*

Through the midseventies, I dealt with these questions, both personally and as an advisor to a largely wealthy secular clientele. In 1977 my wife and I experienced God's call to leave the businesses I was involved in and join a new ministry in Atlanta, Georgia. For two years, as our family grew to five children, I helped to develop seminar materials in the areas of decision making, time management, faith planning, and problem solving. During that time I also traveled to Africa eleven times, assisting a large Christian organization to apply the principles that we were developing.

I observed during all of this that the same financial questions that my former clients and I had been asking were being asked by others as well: missionaries, affluent Africans, poor Africans, full-time Christian workers, successful American executives, pastors, and friends.

- Will I ever have enough?
- Will it continue to be enough?
- How much is enough?

These questions transcend cultures as well as classes.

In 1979, at the encouragement of Dr. Howard Hendricks, I founded an organization called Ronald Blue & Co., which has a simple, yet compelling objective: *to remove the fear and frustration that Christians experience when they deal with money*. The need for this type of counsel and advice is, I believe, pervasive.

Anxiety, worry, guilt, fear—these powerful emotions almost always surround decisions regarding money. Whether dreaming of things desired, struggling to find ways out of budget-busting indebtedness, or questioning how to provide for the future, no one has ever walked into my office or attended one of my seminars completely detached from the emotional issues of financial planning.

Yet Christian teaching and application go from the extreme of sharing personal income in communal living to the "name it and claim it" approach. Both extremes are inadequate from the financial standpoint and the theological perspective. Both are an attempt to *reach* God in the way we handle our money, when all the time *He* is reaching out to us with His wisdom, counsel, and guidance. Unfortunately, much of the teaching Christians receive regarding money management does nothing to alleviate the anxiety that erodes the Christian's peace of mind.

Whatever your personal circumstances, something has made finances a pressing issue for you. Otherwise, you would not be holding this workbook, seeking to make changes in your financial affairs. Perhaps you're having problems repaying a debt. Perhaps you're worried about not having an adequate retirement income. Perhaps you're concerned about providing college educations for your children. Whatever the questions, problems, or concerns, you're doing the right thing by seeking to address your financial situation.

My wife and I began a journey, just as you are beginning one now, to "be filled with the knowledge of His will in all wisdom and spiritual understanding" (Col. 1:9) as we attempted to answer the questions: *Will we ever have enough? How much is enough? What is the appropriate lifestyle for a Christian?* We've found that biblical principles for personal money management are timeless—regardless of changing economic conditions, regardless of our personal situations. The *Master Your Money Workbook* outlines our journey, a journey toward financial freedom, sound stewardship, and responsible money management.

This book is designed to address the nagging anxiety surrounding financial affairs. By providing a framework of financial planning that is both biblical and relevant in our unique society, this ten-week program will enable you to live your life free from the worry, fear, and frustration created by financial uncertainty. By committing to work through this ten-week program, you will:

- Gain an understanding of biblical principles of personal finances;
- Learn the tools to make "order out of chaos";
- Know the criteria for making sound financial decisions;

- Learn to take advantage of inflationary times;
- Develop a plan for getting (and staying) out of debt;
- Identify your long-term and short-term goals;
- Be able to tell when you are on track in meeting your goals;
- Overcome the pitfalls of consumptive spending;
- Learn to live free from financial worry and anxiety.

If these sound like strong promises, you're right. We serve a mighty God and He *wants* us to be free from financial concerns. If we are preoccupied about our financial affairs, we are not free to serve Him. Listening to God's leading in the midst of worry and anxiety is a very difficult, if not impossible, task. When we commit our lives to Christ, we commit our finances as well. No matter what your personal circumstances, *Master Your Money* will provide you with the teaching, the tools, and the techniques to bring order to your finances and peace of mind to your concerns.

As you begin this ten-week program, keep in mind that you are beginning a *process,* a process that takes time, homework, and commitment. You have spent years getting to where you are now financially—ten weeks is a minimal investment for lifetime results.

In more than twenty-five years of helping people plan for their financial future, most of the clients I've served don't arbitrarily decide to seek financial counsel. Developing a financial plan or a family budget is not usually included on someone's list of ten favorite leisure activities! Something prompts their action: a death, a sudden increase or decrease in income, financial difficulties, to name a few. Whatever serves as the catalyst for your decision, I've found it is usually helpful to take a look inward before looking outward. In answering the following questions, try to be as specific as you can without jumping ahead to "solutions."

What in my personal circumstances is causing me the greatest financial anxiety right now? _____

_____

_____

_____

_____

_____

If you will be working through this process with your spouse (which I highly recommend if you are married), does your spouse have a differing view of the situation or problem? _____

_____

_____

_____

_____

Do you see financial obligations arising in the future for which you have no idea how you will provide? (College education, debt repayment, major home repairs, etc.) _____

_____

_____

_____

Do I Need This Program?

"I hate money! No matter how much I earn, I never seem to have enough."

"My husband and I get along great. We don't argue about kids, in-laws, sex—but money—now that's another thing altogether. Money always seems to be a tense subject, so we just avoid talking about it."

"We begin to feel like we're making some progress or getting ahead, then, boom, something unexpected comes up, like major car repairs or having to replace the furnace. It's always something."

"We feel like we're doing okay financially until I begin to think about braces for the kids, college, weddings, retirement. I just don't know how we'll come up with the money when the time comes."

"I know we should give more to our church, but with raising two kids, increasing our tithe just isn't realistic."

"We never use a budget. When we put it all down on paper, we're always in the hole. But somehow, it all seems to work out."

Sound familiar? I've heard comments such as these from hundreds of individuals and couples. Despite the fact that money is merely a means to an end, money is a stressful, highly emotional issue.

Whether trying to make investment decisions or struggling to make ends meet, chances are your decisions about what and how to spend money are shrouded in anxiety, frustration, guilt, or worry. Unfortunately, most of us are lousy money managers, not because we don't want to be good money managers, but because we've never been taught.

Read through these financial facts, and indicate if you think these statements are true (T), false (F), or an exaggerated overstatement (O).

True, False, or Exaggerated?

At age sixty-five:

T F O Nearly half of all Americans are dependent on relatives.

T F O One third of all Americans are dependent on charity.

T F O Nearly one fourth are still working.

T F O Only 2 percent of all Americans ever reach the point of being able to live off the financial resources they've accumulated.

T F O After fifty years of hard work, fewer men are worth $100 at age 68 than at age 18.

T F O The incomes of doctors, lawyers, and most professional people top at age 47 and plunge rapidly after age 54.

T F O Seven out of twelve women will become widows.[1]

T F O The average age of a widow in the United States is fifty-two.

The staggering reality is that all these statements are true.[2] Since 1945 our country has experienced tremendous growth, yet these financial statistics for individuals are sobering. What a tragedy to spend your entire working life and accumulate basically nothing. Yet that is exactly what the greatest majority of Americans are doing.

---

[1]Most statistical sources report that seven out of twelve women will become widows; however, a study appearing in the *Atlanta Journal* reported a substantially higher percentage. The *Atlanta Journal* put the ratio at *eleven out of twelve women become widows.*

[2]Statistics quoted are derived from the Social Security Board, Devney's Economic Tables, and the Department of Commerce.

Too many of us *wait* to plan until it's too *late* to plan. And if we don't plan, we are, by default, planning to fail. In light of these statistics, we know that the vast majority of women will become widows and will be managing inadequate resources. We are setting ourselves up for financial bondage. Let me make this point emphatically: *Failing to plan is, in reality, planning to fail.*

A significant part of the problem behind these financial statistics is this: *80 percent of Americans owe more than they own.* Quite simply, if you added up all their assets and all their liabilities, they'd have more liabilities than assets. Repayment of debt consumes 25 percent of all incomes today, not including mortgage debt. When mortgage debt is added to that figure, a staggering 50 percent of all incomes today goes toward indebtedness. Most people don't realize where they stand financially and, therefore, don't know they're headed for trouble.

Time for Honesty with Myself

Enough said about these statistics. What about your situation? Ask yourself the following questions and circle your answer. If you find yourself answering yes to more than three, you are taking the right step by choosing to work through this planning process.

- Yes   No   Have you and your spouse ever argued over financial matters?

- Yes   No   Have you ever impulsively purchased a car or major appliance?

- Yes   No   Do you routinely fail to reconcile your checking account?

- Yes   No   Do you overdraft your checking account more than once or twice a year, or frequently go into a checking account credit line to avoid overdrafts?

- Yes   No   Have you tried sticking to a budget before, but given up after only a few weeks or months?

- Yes   No   Do you occasionally or frequently receive past due notices?

- Yes   No   Do you use credit cards for emergency expenses (car repairs, unexpected travel expenses, etc.)?

- Yes   No   Are your credit cards at or near the credit limit?
- Yes   No   Do you use your credit cards to meet household living expenses (such as purchasing groceries, eating out, etc.)?
- Yes   No   Do you routinely pay only the minimum amount due on credit accounts?
- Yes   No   Have you considered, applied for, or received a consolidation loan?
- Yes   No   Do you frequently dip into savings to meet expenses?
- Yes   No   Do you have *less than* three months worth of living expenses in cash available in savings or money market funds?
- Yes   No   Have you ever borrowed money from parents, other relatives, or friends and failed to repay the loan according to the agreed terms?
- Yes   No   Does the level of your mortgage cause you uneasiness, anxiety, or insomnia?
- Yes   No   Have you had any bills turned over to a collection agency?

If you answered yes to more than half of these questions, this planning process is critical to your long- and short-term financial stability. The sooner you address your financial situation, the better. I'll say again, *failing to plan is planning to fail.* Using the principles, tools, and techniques outlined in this workbook, you will change your financial situation significantly in the next ten weeks.

COMMIT TO SUCCESS

The first step in the financial planning process, and possibly the most important step, is your commitment to work the program. If you commit to the program and faithfully work the plan, you can trust the results to God. No matter what your present situation is, God is bigger than your financial concerns.

I encourage you to make a commitment to God, your spouse, and yourself to this ten-week process. If your spouse is unwilling or unable to participate with you or if you are single, you may find it helpful to ask someone to "partner" with you in this process; you will find a partnership with a friend or trusted confidant to be a source of support and encouragement as well as an effective technique for maintaining personal accountability.

Another helpful technique is to establish a specific time each week for financial planning. If you were to enroll in a college course or seminar, you probably wouldn't schedule a conflicting engagement during the class time. So too with this program—make a commitment to yourself to hold this time inviolate. Initially, during this ten-week program, your weekly sessions will require one to two hours. However, once your financial plan is in place, no more than twenty to thirty minutes will be required. Eventually, *you will be spending no more than an hour or so a month to keep on track with your financial plan*. The initial ten-week investment will pay off long-term dividends, both financially and emotionally. You owe it to yourself (and your family) to make this a priority.

A Commitment to Plan

I, _____, recognize that if I don't begin a process of financial planning, I am, by default, planning to fail. I also recognize that the time is now—I can no longer allow other obligations and commitments to take priority over addressing my financial situation. By God's grace and with His guidance, I commit to following the *Master Your Money* financial planning process.

My weekly financial planning session will be on (day) _____ at (time) _____. If an unavoidable emergency arises which preempts this time, I will arrange an alternate time for that week as a "make-up" session.

I will ask _____ to partner with me in this process. I will schedule my first planning session for _____; and I will conclude the workbook planning sessions on _____.

Signed _____

Date _____

THREE KEYS TO GUARANTEED SUCCESS: <u>WHAT NOT TO DO</u>

First, remember you are beginning a process, not a project. As you work through the process, *don't strive for perfection*—there is no such thing. Shoot for 80 percent accuracy.

Second, in financial planning, *don't focus on the past*. Isaiah 43:18 says, "Do not remember the former things, / Nor consider the things of old." Focusing on the past tends to limit our thinking to our past experiences and our past failures. More importantly, focusing on the past leaves God out of the process. "Now to Him who is able to do exceedingly abundantly above all that we ask or think, according to the power that works in us" (Eph. 3:20). God is never limited by what has gone on in the past, and wants to do something beyond what we can even think or imagine.

Third, *don't try to "fix" your financial situation overnight*. Give yourself time—working through the entire process is critical to achieving long-term changes in your financial situation.

<u>YOU CAN HAVE ENOUGH</u>

From a financial standpoint, you *can* have enough. If you plan, using the principles and techniques presented in this workbook, you will have enough. However, most of us have difficulty believing this is possible because our security comes from money. If our security comes from money, we'll never have enough. I don't care how much you have, it will never be enough. This is the reason the *Master Your Money* process is founded on biblical principles. Without an understanding of our scriptural foundation, of what God is calling us to do and where our security truly lies, the financial planning process is of no more value than arithmetic gymnastics. The first week of this program will focus on four biblical principles.

PART TWO

The 10-Week Program to Master Your Money

WEEK ONE

What Is Success?

Four Biblical Principles of Money Management

Bob and Laura were visibly nervous as they walked into my office. An attractive couple, they had been married twenty years and had two children, a son in college and a sixteen-year-old daughter, Sue. Bob was considering going into business for himself, a dream he had longed to pursue for years—but one he had postponed due to family responsibilities and financial obligations.

"This is an opportunity of a lifetime," Bob said emphatically after they had briefly explained why they were seeking my counsel. "If I don't do it now, I don't think I ever will. But Laura has a negative reaction every time we even *talk* about the possibility."

"I just don't see how we can do it," Laura quickly said. "Friends who've gone into business for themselves say they wish they had started with twice as much capital—and made much more conservative revenue projections. I love this man I married, but he's such an optimist! If he quits his job now, what assurances do we have for our income? This time when he raised the question of going on his own, it was less than half an hour after he told our daughter, Sue, that we couldn't afford to send her on a church-sponsored ski trip she's wanted to go on for four years. If we can't afford that, how can we afford this?''

Bob and Laura's situation is typical of many married couples. They had reached an impasse: Bob's adamant determination to pursue his dream of being his own boss—and Laura's equally determined ''intuition'' that the decision wasn't ''right'' for them. In a tense truce, they made the decision to seek outside counsel.

With one child in college, another soon to be, and facing the major financial implications of a difficult decision, their financial conflict was not at all unusual. One of the greatest causes of marital conflict in our country is money. When you put two people together with differing desires and priorities, there's going to be conflict. But marriages don't end because of money problems. Money is nothing more than a tool to meet certain needs, goals, or objectives. The real issue for Bob and Laura, as it is for you and your spouse, is to ask, ''As we live together as a couple, how do we work together financially?''

Everyone, whether married or single, Christian or non-Christian, is concerned with success, with making the ''right'' choices and decisions. Yet how I define ''success'' becomes the key factor in knowing what the ''right'' choices are, in knowing when I've achieved success. Without a common framework, a common understanding of how sound financial decisions are to be made, most couples will experience conflicting needs, desires, and priorities when facing financial issues.

We live in the most affluent society in the world, where many individuals have ''successful'' careers, incomes, and lifestyles, yet very few of these same individuals manage their money—their money manages them.

At a speaking engagement in Newport Beach, California, I was introduced to the group by a man who began by saying, ''Here in Newport Beach we live in million-dollar homes, vacation in Hawaii, we drive Mercedes and BMWs, and we hide when the paperboy comes by to collect.'' Surprising? Not really. Not in a society where billions of dollars are spent annually by advertisers enticing us to buy things we don't really need.

When I asked my oldest daughter how her friends would define success, she gave me the best worldly definition of success I have ever heard: ''To have whatever you want, whenever you want it.''

What is success? And more importantly, what is success for a Christian? Before you can make sound financial decisions, you have to reach an understanding of what "success" means for you, as a Christian, as an individual, and as a couple.

For many Christians, spending patterns are in conflict with values; in other words, what you *believe* is important may not be reflected in how your money is actually spent. This incongruence is frequently one of the causes of the emotional anxiety, frustration, and guilt surrounding financial matters. Psychologists call this incongruence between values (what you believe is important) and behavior (what your actions demonstrate) "value conflict." Before looking at the four biblical principles of money management, let's spend some time clarifying what's important to you.

Looking at What You Value

Money is a resource you use to accomplish the desires you have. Read through this list, prioritizing the list according to what you value and desire. Put a 1 by the one thing most important to you, a 2 by the second most important, etc.

_____ Security   _____ Properly trained children

_____ Peace   _____ Contentment

_____ Flexibility   _____ Comfort

_____ Physical fitness   _____ Obedience to God

_____ Transportation   _____ Rest and relaxation

_____ Self-worth   _____ Acceptance

_____ Sense of belonging   _____ Appearance

_____ Personal/spiritual
      growth

      Others:

_____ _____

_____ _____

_____ _____

_____ _____

We will come back to this list later during this session, to see how our spending decisions integrate these values.

FOUR BIBLICAL PRINCIPLES
OF MONEY MANAGEMENT

The Bible has a lot to say about money. Over 2,000 verses deal with money and possessions; there are only 500 verses on prayer. Five times more is said in the Bible about money than prayer! And in the Gospels, 16 out of 38 parables deal with money. Obviously, there are a few things God wants us to understand about money.

Although the parable of the talents does not deal primarily with money, it does illustrate four basic biblical principles summarizing much of what the Bible has to say regarding money and money management. So let's begin there.

Read the parable of the talents from Matthew 25:14–30:

> For the kingdom of heaven is like a man traveling to a far country, who called his own servants and delivered his goods to them. And to one he gave five talents, to another two, and to another one, to each according to his own ability; and immediately he went on a journey.
>
> Then he who had received the five talents went and traded with them, and made another five talents. And likewise he who had received two gained two more also. But he who had received one went and dug in the ground, and hid his lord's money.
>
> After a long time the lord of those servants came and settled accounts with them. So he who had received five talents came and brought five other talents, saying, "Lord, you delivered to me five talents; look, I have gained five more talents besides them."
>
> His lord said to him, "Well done, good and faithful servant; you were faithful over a few things, I will make you ruler over many things. Enter into the joy of your lord."
>
> He also who had received two talents came and said, "Lord, you delivered to me two talents; look, I have gained two more talents besides them."
>
> His lord said to him, "Well done, good and faithful servant; you have been faithful over a few things, I will make you ruler over many things. Enter into the joy of your lord."
>
> Then he who had received the one talent came and said, "Lord, I knew you to be a hard man, reaping where you have not sown, and

gathering where you have not scattered seed. And I was afraid, and went and hid your talent in the ground. Look, there you have what is yours."

But his lord answered and said to him, "You wicked and lazy servant, you knew that I reap where I have not sown, and gather where I have not scattered seed. So you ought to have deposited my money with the bankers, and at my coming I would have received back my own with interest. Therefore take the talent from him, and give it to him who has ten talents. For to everyone who has, more will be given, and he will have abundance; but from him who does not have, even what he has will be taken away. And cast the unprofitable servant into the outer darkness. There will be weeping and gnashing of teeth."

Biblical Principle #1: God Owns It All

For the kingdom of heaven is like a man traveling to a far country, who called his own servants and delivered his goods to them.
—Matthew 25:14

In the verse above, the key phrase is emphasized. God owns it all. The goods are His to do with as He wills.

Very few Christians would argue with the principle that God owns it all, and yet if we follow this principle to its natural conclusion, we find two life-changing implications.

First, God has the right to whatever He wants, whenever He wants it. It is all His. An owner has *rights,* and I, as a steward, have only *responsibilities*.

When my oldest daughter reached driving age, she was very eager to use my car, which I willingly allowed her to do. There was never any question that I could take back my car at any time for any reason. She had only responsibilities, while I maintained all the rights. In the same way, every single possession that I have comes from God. *I literally possess much, but own nothing*.

The second implication of God's owning it all is this: not only is my giving or tithing a spiritual decision, but *every* spending decision is a spiritual decision. There is nothing more spiritual than buying a car, taking a vacation, buying food, paying off debt, paying taxes, and so on. These are all uses of His resources. He owns all that I have. The Bible reveals many specific guidelines as to how the Owner wants His property used. As a steward, I have a great deal of latitude, but I am still responsible to the Owner.

If God Owns It All, What Does That Mean for Me?

Think about these implications:

- I possess much but own nothing—God owns it all.
- Every spending decision is a spiritual decision.

Walk around your property and home to get a feel for the reality of this principle. Reflect on how long the dirt has been there and how long it will continue to be there. Ask yourself if you really own it or whether you merely possess it. You may have the title to it, but that title reflects your right to possess it temporarily, not forever. Only God literally owns it forever. Think about the freedom of knowing that if God owns it all—and He does—He must have some thoughts about how He wants me to use His property. Then come back and write down your thoughts and reflections.

_____

_____

_____

_____

_____

_____

_____

_____

_____

_____

_____

_____

_____

_____

Biblical Principle #2: We Are in a Growth Process

His lord said to him, "Well done, good and faithful servant; you were faithful over a few things, I will make you ruler over many things. Enter into the joy of your lord."

—Matthew 25:21

The Scriptures clearly tell us that our time on earth is temporary and is to be used as a training time. This message in the parable of the talents is inescapable. During this growth process, God uses money and material possessions as *a tool, a test, and a testimony*.

My role as a financial advisor is to help you discover what God would have you learn, either from your financial abundance or apparent lack of financial resources. God is not trying to frustrate you; God is trying to get your attention—and money is a great attention getter.

Money is not only a tool, but also a test in managing someone else's resources. If your checkbook precedes you to Heaven could you confidently expect God to say as you stood before Him, "Well done, good and faithful servant"? Is that hope unrealistic? Not at all. It is God's desire and intention—He wants it more than you do.

Finally, God can use *my* use of His resources as a testimony to the world. My attitude as a Christian toward wealth becomes a part of my testimony.

God has called us to be salt and light. "You are the salt of the earth; but if the salt loses its flavor, how shall it be seasoned? It is then good for nothing but to be thrown out and trampled under foot by men. You are the light of the world. A city that is set on a hill cannot be hidden" (Matt. 5:13–14).

God wants me to be, as salt and light, not *better* than, but *different* from. As Christians, we may or may not have more than our neighbors, but that does not distinguish us from anyone. What does distinguish Christians from the world is *the absence of any financial anxiety,* because the world and its temporal possessions do not possess us. The Christian is prayerful but not anxious about the tremendous uncertainty facing our national and world economy.

Obviously, that attitude is not "normal" but rather "different," and it comes from having an entirely different perspective. As Christians, we know that God owns it all, that God is in control. Our perspective is eternal, giving us the freedom to have an attitude of holding possessions lightly. Truly, that is different!

Not only have we been called to be salt and light, but we have been called to be *servants*. "For even the Son of Man did not come to be served, but to serve, and to give His life a ransom for many," says Mark 10:45. Money is one of the most significant resources with which American Christians can serve others. It is not the only resource—time and talents are two others—but it is certainly in greater abundance among American Christians than among non-Americans.

Looking at My Finances from a Spiritual Perspective

Recognizing that your finances are a tool, a test, and a testimony, ask yourself these questions and record your reflections:

Have you ever had a major financial disappointment or setback? If so, describe the situation and how you felt: _____

_____

_____

_____

Did you wonder if, or ask yourself why, God had failed to answer your prayers? _____

Read these two verses and complete the following statement.

For God so loved the world that He gave His only begotten Son, that whoever believes in Him should not perish but have everlasting life.
—John 3:16

For I know the thoughts that I think toward you, says the LORD, thoughts of peace and not of evil, to give you a future and a hope. Then you will call upon Me and go and pray to Me, and I will listen to you. And you will seek Me and find Me, when you search for Me with all your heart.
—Jeremiah 29:11–13

Knowing that God is a loving God and is concerned about my welfare, I think He may have been using the situation to teach me _____

Biblical Principle #3: The Amount Is Not Important

Reread Matthew 25:20–23:

> So he who had received five talents came and brought five other talents, saying, "Lord, you delivered to me five talents; look, I have gained five more talents besides them." His lord said to him, "Well done, good and faithful servant; you were faithful over a few things, I will make you ruler over many things. Enter into the joy of your lord." He also who had received two talents came and said, "Lord, you delivered to me two talents; look, I have gained two more talents besides them." His lord said to him, "Well done, good and faithful servant; you have been faithful over a few things, I will make you ruler over many things. Enter into the joy of your lord."

Compare verse 21 to verse 23, word for word. What differences, if any, are there between the two verses? _____

_____

_____

When you look back at verse 21 and compare it to verse 23, you will see that the same words were spoken to the servant with five talents and the one with two talents. Both were reminded that they had been faithful with a few things and both were promised rewards. The owner makes no distinction between the greater and lesser amounts. The principle for us is simple: The amount we have is unimportant, but how we handle what we've been entrusted with is very important.

Controversy abounds today about whether a Christian is "more spiritual" by accumulating much or by giving it all away. Both perspectives are extremes, and neither reflects the principles I find in the Bible. God doesn't condemn wealth and commend poverty, or vice versa. The principle found in Scripture is that He owns it all. Therefore, whatever He chooses to entrust you with, hold with an open hand, allowing Him to entrust you with more if He so chooses, or allowing Him to take whatever He wants. It is all His. That is the attitude He wants to develop in you, whatever you have, little or much.

Giving Ownership Back to God

On the next page, list those assets that have a unique or special value to you. For example, picture in your mind your home, one room at a time, and recall those things you hold dear. This may include antiques, jewelry, items of furniture, collectables, etc. It may also include your right to own a home, your job, or any desires you may have for the future.

After listing these items, take a moment (for couples, husband and wife together) and surrender these things to God to use and do with as He pleases in your life. Sign and date the deed. This is the first step of recognizing God's ownership.

If at any time you begin to feel anxious about any of these items, simply look back to this deed where you gave them away. No sense in getting anxious about what is not yours.

He is no fool who gives up what he cannot keep to gain what he cannot lose.
—Jim Elliott

Deed of Surrender

On this date I/we acknowledge God's ownership and my/our stewardship responsibility of the following:

ITEM   AMOUNT

_____

_____

_____

_____

_____

_____

_____

_____

_____

_____

_____

_____

_____

_____

_____

Date _____

_____
Signature

_____
Signature

Biblical Principle #4: Faith Requires Action

Then he who had received the one talent came and said, "Lord, I knew you to be a hard man, reaping where you have not sown, and gathering where you have not scattered seed. And I was afraid, and went and hid your talent in the ground. Look, there you have what is yours." But his lord answered and said to him, "You wicked and lazy servant, you knew that I reap where I have not sown, and gather where I have not scattered seed. So you ought to have deposited my money with the bankers, and at my coming I would have received back my own with interest. Therefore take the talent from him, and give it to him who has ten talents. For to everyone who has, more will be given, and he will have abundance; but from him who does not have, even what he has will be taken away. And cast the unprofitable servant into the outer darkness. There will be weeping and gnashing of teeth."

—Matthew 25:24–30

The fourth principle we learn from this parable is clear: God is calling us to be stewards, and as His stewards, our faith requires action. The wicked servant knew what was expected of him, but he *did* nothing. Many of us know what we ought to do, but we don't do it. We have emotional faith and/or intellectual faith, but not volitional faith.

We know, *but* . . .

We may know deep down what God would have us do, but we are so bombarded with worldly input that we are paralyzed. We take no action because we fear making a mistake, biblically or financially. Or we are frustrated and confused. We do only what we feel good about—and living by our feelings will never provide the basis for sound financial decisions.

So grab your checkbook and take a look at what it reveals. A life story could be written from a checkbook. Your checkbook reflects your goals, priorities, convictions, relationships, and even the use of your time. Every area of the Christian life can be faked—except stewardship. Even a person who has been a Christian only a short time can fake prayer, Bible study, evangelism, and going to church, but you can't fake what your checkbook reveals.

Checkbook Inventory

Go back to the exercise on page 19 ("Looking at What You Value"). Take your top five priorities from the list (those you rated 1–5) and write them in the category spaces at the top of the chart on page 30. Then flip through the entries from the past one to two weeks in your checkbook and write the nature of the expense under "Expense Description" and the amount under the category representing the need, desire, or value each expenditure reflects. The purpose of this exercise is to clarify whether your expenditures are in keeping with your values. Don't spend a great deal of time on this exercise— shoot for 80 percent accuracy.

Example: Laura's top five priorities were (1) security; (2) personal/ spiritual growth; (3) properly trained children; (4) obedience to God; (5) healthy marriage. Look at her entries on page 29.

Now go back through your checkbook, listing the expenditures under the appropriate value or priority category on page 30. This exercise need not be exhaustive; just as Laura's entries indicate, you will quickly see if your spending is in keeping with your values.

Category	Security	Growth	Children training	Obedience to God	Marriage	Other Value
Expense Description						
Best Reflections (hair appointment)						$45.00
Lake Harriet Dance (girls' ballet lessons)			$55.00			
Cash (lunch while shopping)						$20.00
Rainbow Food (groceries)						$85.00
Logos (Bible study materials)		$15.00				
State Farm Insur.	$95.00					

Most people are surprised by the results of this simple exercise. Don't be discouraged if you find a great disparity between what you prioritized as your values and your actual expenditures. The financial planning framework you will be developing during the next nine weeks will:

- Give you a process for managing your money;
- Summarize the almost infinite alternative uses of money into just a manageable few;
- Integrate long-range goals (what you value and desire) with short-range needs and commitments;
- Give you a means of prioritizing your financial decisions;
- Remove some of the guilt, confusion, and anxiety that surround money.

We've spent this session learning the four biblical principles of money management for one very important reason: these principles are the corner-

Category						Other Value
Expense Description						

stone of financial success, a critical foundation for all your future financial decisions. We began this session by asking, What is success? And for those who are married, the question of success must be considered by answering this question: As we live together as a couple, how do we work together financially? Through working the *Master Your Money* planning process, you will be able to answer these questions for yourself. But before moving ahead to the final section of this session, let's review the biblical imperative.

The Bottom Line of the Biblical Call

No matter what your beliefs and attitudes regarding money have been in the past, the biblical call is clear:

- In Matthew 5:13–16, God is calling us to be salt and light (not better than, but different from the world around us);
- In Mark 10:45, God is calling us to be servants;
- In Matthew 25:14–30, God is calling us to be stewards.

As His stewards, we will begin to integrate four biblical principles into all our financial affairs:

- God owns it all;
- We are in a growth process;
- The amount we have is not important; how we use that amount is very important;
- Faith requires action.

During Bob and Laura's first financial-planning sessions, Bob was eager to get on with the "number crunching" of financial planning. After reviewing the four biblical principles, he asked a very pertinent question.

"I can accept these principles," he said, "but how do we put these principles into action? How does this make a difference in trying to decide whether or not to buy a business, or where to find the money to send Sue on the mission trip?"

Putting these principles into action is what *Master Your Money* is designed to accomplish. Before concluding this first week's session, however, we need to clarify several basic objectives of financial planning.

A FINANCIAL PLANNING OVERVIEW

Ultimately, financial planning is the predetermined use of financial resources in order to accomplish certain goals and objectives. The difference between the Christian and the non-Christian in financial planning is the source of the goals and objectives. An acquaintance of mine, William C. Cook, wrote a book called *Success, Motivation and the Scriptures,* in which he defined success as "the continued achievement of God-given goals." Success is knowing what God would have you to be and do and how to achieve that, so that when you stand before Him, you will hear Him say, "Well done, good and faithful servant."

Our working definition for success is quite simple: Success is knowing where you are going in life and knowing how to get there. Money, then, is one of the resources you use to accomplish your goals, to "achieve success." For the Christian, accumulating financial resources should never be an end in itself. When money becomes our focus, we are doomed to disappointment, because it is merely a resource and was never intended by the Creator to be anything more than that.

Financial Planning Diagram

Look now at the Financial Planning Diagram on the opposite page. This diagram illustrates that all our spending decisions meet either short-term needs or long-term goals. From a short-term perspective, there are only five alternative uses for all income coming into a household:

1. Given away;
2. Spent to support lifestyle;
3. Used for the repayment of debt;
4. Used to meet tax obligations;
5. Accumulated or saved (cash-flow margin).

From a long-term standpoint, there are only six financial possibilities or objectives:

1. Financial independence;
2. College education for children;
3. Paying off debt;

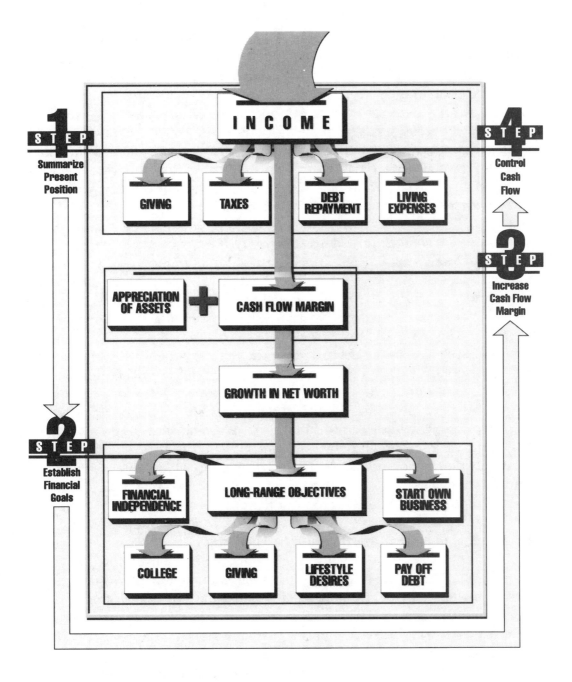

4. Major lifestyle desires;
5. Major charitable giving;
6. Owning your own business.

As you review the diagram, there are three significant implications to consider. First, there are no independent financial decisions. *Every spending decision or use of money accomplishes one of these eleven objectives*. If you make a decision to use financial resources in any one area, by definition, you have chosen not to use those same resources in the other areas. This means that if you choose to set aside money for college education or financial independence, you no longer have that money available to spend on giving, lifestyle desires, debt repayment, and the like. Likewise, if you decide to spend money on lifestyle desires, you no longer have those same resources available for any other short-term need or long-term goal.

Second, *the longer-term your perspective, the better the possibility of your making a good financial decision now*. There are always more alternative uses of money than there is money available. *No matter what your situation, no matter what your income level,* there are always more alternative uses of money than there is money available. How money is allocated among the five short-term alternatives is a function of just two factors: the *commitments* I already have and my *priorities*. As a father of five children, I have certain lifestyle commitments that someone with fewer children, or no children, does not have. Debt repayment, taxes, and giving are all commitments I must maintain. Certain lifestyle expenses such as utilities, food, insurance, etc., are also commitments. A commitment must always be top priority.

My priorities will dictate the allocation of the balance of my resources. Giving and accumulation (savings) are usually stated as priorities, but in reality, usually they wind up at the bottom of the priority ladder. In working with hundreds of clients at all income levels, I have observed that most American Christians have lifestyle as their top priority and second, because of their lifestyle, debt repayment. Taxes become the third priority, because they have no choice; accumulation is fourth; and finally, giving.

The Bible gives us many guidelines about each of the five short-term uses of money, but very little in the way of direct commandment. To determine what God would have us do in balancing our commitments with our priorities requires the discipline of spending time with Him. No one other person, including a financial planner, can tell you how to prioritize your spending. Why? God has not entrusted the resources you possess (but do not own) to someone else; only you are accountable for managing the use of God's resources entrusted to you.

The third implication of the Financial Planning Diagram is *the lifetime nature of financial decisions*. Of the five short-range uses of money, three are consumptive in nature and two are productive. Lifestyle expenditures, debt repayment, and taxes are all consumptive in nature; when the money is spent, it is gone. Any time money is used consumptively, it can never be used again for anything in the future. Both accumulation and giving are productive uses of money. Money that is put into accumulation is much like planting a crop—later on, much more than what was planted comes up and can be used again for either consumption or production. Our spending decisions today determine our financial tomorrow. Once I make a decision to either save or spend, I have determined to some extent my destiny. My financial decisions determine my destiny.

There is tremendous freedom of mind in knowing and believing that God owns it all, and that money is nothing more than a resource provided by God to allow us to accomplish His purposes on this earth. How to achieve one or more long-term goals, such as financial independence, college education, getting out of debt, or starting our own business, is simple, but very few Americans do it: *spend less than you earn and do it for a long time.*

A retired pastor who never earned more than $8,000 a year came to see me when he was eighty years old, wanting to know if he had enough financial resources to live out the rest of his life. At the time he came in to my office, he had been retired for twenty years and his wife had just been put under full-time nursing care.

As I generally do, I began asking some questions before giving him any advice. First, I asked him if he had any debts.

"No," he replied. "I've never borrowed any money."

"Why not?" I asked, surprised by his response.

"Well, I knew if I borrowed money," he said, "I would have to pay it back someday, and I never could afford to pay it back, feed my family, and tithe."

Then I asked him what resources he presently had. He told me that in his wife's name, he had approximately $250,000 in cash, money-market funds, and certificates of deposit. Additionally, in his name, he had another $350,000 in cash and cash-type investments. Needless to say, I was impressed! Over $600,000 in cash accumulated by a couple who had never earned more than $8,000 per year!

One thing bothered me though. He had not mentioned any stock investments, and yet in looking at his tax returns, I noticed a substantial amount of dividend income. When I questioned him about the dividend income, he revealed that at retirement he had invested $10,000 in the stock of a new company, and at the present time, the market value of his stock was $1,063,000.

WOW! $1,663,000 of cash and stock and they had never earned more than $8,000 per year!

Needless to say, this couple is unusual; they tithed, paid their taxes, and lived on what was left. But many of the couples with whom I've worked are headed in the same direction. By practicing the four biblical principles we've covered during this session, and working through the *Master Your Money* planning process, you'll find these principles will work for you, too, regardless of the uncertainty of our economic environment.

WEEK TWO
Where Am I?

Determining Net Worth

"How can we make so much money and never have any?" Laura asked. "Our boat payment is habitually late. We go from one pay period to the next, always feeling like it's spent before we ever deposit Bob's check. When Bob talks about quitting his job, I get a knot in my stomach. I just don't think we can afford to make a mistake."

"But she won't even give me a chance," Bob said. Angry and frustrated, Bob *knew* he could make a go of it on his own. Laura wasn't convinced.

Laura's hesitation and uneasiness with making a major decision that would have a significant impact on their current financial situation was justifiable. To know conclusively where you are financially is absolutely necessary before you can even *begin* to plan for the accomplishment of goals, dreams, and desires. More so than simply filling out the required information necessary for a small business loan, developing a sound financial plan takes into consideration all aspects of your lifestyle, short-term commitments, and long-term goals. The first step in financial planning is determining exactly where you are now. At the conclusion of this week's session, you will have answered the question "Where am I?" by working through four financial summaries:

1. An inventory of your assets and liabilities;
2. A statement of your net worth;
3. An evaluation of your likelihood to borrow and accumulate;
4. A determination of your income available for lifestyle.

STATEMENT OF NET WORTH

A statement of net worth is much like a snapshot or X-ray. It gives a summary of every financial decision that has been made, but it summarizes those financial transactions at a specific point in time. Specifically, a statement of net worth lists all of the assets that are owned, then subtracts from that listing of assets all of the liabilities (debts owed); and the resulting number is one's net worth.

Typically, after high school or college, young people go to work and find that their income does not support their needs. They borrow to fund some of their desires and needs—an automobile, some furniture, a home, and maybe even further education. If they add up what they have accumulated in the way of cash, investments, furniture, cars, and homes, they will have the total of all they own. However, they may have a substantial amount of debt which, when subtracted from what they own, leaves a small or even a negative net worth situation.

By adding up all of your assets and subtracting all liabilities, you can get a summary of net worth at any time. This one number is a summary of every financial transaction ever entered into. The objective is to have that number growing in size relative to your life's goals. Unfortunately, what most frequently happens is that once established in a career with a home, children, pets, and white picket fence, few couples regularly review a statement of their net worth until a major financial decision or crisis arises.

The value of a net worth statement becomes clear when you examine the finances of Bob and Laura. Whether or not to go into business for himself was not the only financial question they needed to face. They also needed to address questions such as how much and where to give, how to reduce taxes, how much life insurance to own, how to reduce their debt, and what investments made sense for them—all valid questions, all major considerations financially. Knowing where you are by preparing a statement of net worth is the first step in developing your financial plan.

When preparing a statement of net worth,[1] assets are to be listed at a value they could be sold for and liabilities are to be listed at the current balance due. Here's how Bob and Laura's assets and liabilities looked:

---

[1] A statement of net worth will usually include a review of your current life insurance. You will be analyzing your life insurance needs and evaluating your current life insurance during Week Nine.

A Review of Bob & Laura's Finances

Assets

Liquid

Cash on hand and checking account	$ 2,000.00
Money market funds	—
CDs (____% interest rate)	—
Savings (6% interest rate)	1,000.00
Marketable securities	—
Life insurance cash values	6,000.00
Other assets:	—
	—
	—
Total liquid assets	$ 9,000.00

Nonliquid:

Home (market value)	$112,000.00
Land (market value)	—
Business valuation	—
Real estate investments	15,000.00
Limited partnerships	—
Boat, camper, tractor, etc.	6,000.00
Automobile(s) (market value)	8,000.00
Furniture and personal property (estimated market value)	5,000.00
Coin & stamp collections, antiques, etc.	—
IRA's, Keogh	—
Pension & profit sharing	—
Receivables from others	—
Other	—
Total nonliquid assets	$146,000.00

Liabilities

	Creditor	Balance Due	Interest Rate	Payment Schedule Per month	Until when
1.	Charge cards	$ 3,000	18%	$ 50	Forever
2.	Auto loans	6,000	12%	263	3 yrs
3.	Parents	5,000	6%	—	?
4.	Boat loan	5,000	14%	200	3 yrs
5.	Bank loan	13,500	15%	200	10 yrs
6.	Life insurance	5,000	5%	—	?
7.	Home mortgage	81,500	9%	684	25 yrs
8.					
9.					
10.					
	Totals	**$119,000**		**$1,397**	

To come up with their net worth, we subtract the total balance owed of $119,000 from the total of liquid and nonliquid assets of $155,000 to show them that they now have a net worth of $36,000. So what does this mean?

It means that they had some problems in their financial situation, problems which they were completely unaware of. They also had some strengths that could be used to their advantage—and they need to take some action. However, before analyzing their assets and liabilities, complete your own inventory of assets and liabilities.

As you list your assets, the following pointers help clarify some of your questions about assets.

- Liquid assets are those assets that could be converted into cash immediately, with no loss of principal or penalty.
- Use fair market values when listing your assets (what you think they would be worth if sold today).
- If you do not know the fair market value, you should use the original cost value.
- You should not list the net values of investments and real estate owned since the liability will be listed under the liabilities section.
- Stocks and bonds are liquid assets (marketable securities) and should be listed at fair market value.
- Individual Retirement Accounts are considered nonliquid assets since there is a penalty for premature withdrawal.

- List pension and profit-sharing accounts only if the fund is actually yours and could be taken with you or liquidated at your choice. In determining the value, use the vested amount that would come to you today. If there are no lump sum options, then no value should be listed. Pension and retirement plans are non-liquid assets only if you have the right to withdraw them without penalty. (In other words, they are assets that you have funded personally and not a company-funded contribution, which will be taxed if withdrawn prematurely.)
- Business valuations can be at the current book value as determined by the latest financial statements or perhaps a multiple of business earnings, e.g., five times the average earnings over the last three years.
- Life insurance cash value is the cash surrender value. Any loans against the cash values should be listed as a liability.

The following pointers may help clarify any questions you may have concerning liabilities.

- As a matter of convenience you may want to list long-term debts first (for example, your home mortgage).
- Do not include utility bills and monthly bills as a liability since these will be addressed next week when you develop a cash-flow summary.
- If you are behind on mortgage payments, then list the amounts you are in arrears as a debt that is due.

Inventory Your Assets

Liquid:

Cash on hand and checking account	$_____
Money market funds	_____
CDs (____% interest rate)	_____
Savings (____% interest rate)	_____
Marketable securities	_____
Life insurance cash values	_____
Other _____	_____
Other _____	_____
Total liquid assets	$_____

Nonliquid:

Home (market value)	$_____
Land (market value)	_____
Business valuation	_____
Real estate investments	_____
Limited partnerships	_____
Boat, camper, tractor, etc.	_____
Automobile(s) (market value)	_____
Furniture and personal property (estimated market value)	_____
Coin & stamp collections, antiques, etc.	_____
IRA's, Keogh	_____
Pension & profit sharing	_____
Receivables from others	_____
Other _____	_____

Total nonliquid assets $_____

Inventory Your Liabilities

	Creditor	Balance Due	Interest Rate	Payment Schedule Per month	Until when
1.	_____	$_____	_____	$_____	_____
2.	_____	_____	_____	_____	_____
3.	_____	_____	_____	_____	_____
4.	_____	_____	_____	_____	_____
5.	_____	_____	_____	_____	_____
6.	_____	_____	_____	_____	_____
7.	_____	_____	_____	_____	_____
8.	_____	_____	_____	_____	_____
9.	_____	_____	_____	_____	_____
10.	_____	_____	_____	_____	_____
Totals		$_____	_____	$_____	_____

Once we've completed an inventory of assets and liabilities, we are ready to determine your net worth by preparing a personal balance sheet. A personal balance sheet includes several indicators that give us a measurement of financial health. Before reviewing Bob and Laura's personal balance sheet, let's define the key indicators in a statement of net worth.

Liquid Assets

When preparing a statement of net worth, one major category of assets is those that are liquid—those that could be turned into cash immediately. The person who has liquidity has financial flexibility to meet emergencies, unexpected bills, make major purchases, and take advantage of opportunities that come along. The more liquid the finances, the more flexible the person is— and probably more financially secure. However, there is a risk of having all of one's resources be liquid, that is, in the bank or in cash or cash-type investments. These risks will be covered in Week Eight: Growth Strategies and Investment Opportunities.

Productive Assets

The next category on your personal balance sheet will be those assets that are productive, meaning an asset that has the potential to generate income for investment purposes. Bob and Laura's listing of productive assets includes all of the liquid assets plus the real estate investment, for a total of $24,000. Some of their other assets may grow in value, such as their home, but that was not their primary reason for purchasing a home. The purpose of the home is to have a place to live, and it is typically not sold merely to produce income.

In comparing Bob and Laura's total productive assets of $24,000 to their total assets of $155,000, a rather typical picture emerges of a young couple who have invested, over time, their excess cash flow for the most part in personal-type assets as opposed to investment assets or productive assets. If they continue to follow the usual pattern as they grow older, the amount of their productive assets will grow in relation to their total assets, because accumulation needs are generally met sometime between the ages of thirty-five and fifty. After that point, the primary emphasis is on accumulating assets that can be used to fund retirement when it comes.

Propensity to Borrow

Bob and Laura have a strong propensity to borrow—that is, their liabilities divided by their assets reveal they are 77 percent likely to borrow in order to accumulate. In other words, 77 percent of their assets have been accumulated by borrowing rather than by generating a positive cash-flow margin. The lower the percentage of borrowing to accumulate, the better the financial situation is. Zero percent means that there has been no borrowing to accumulate; 100 percent or greater means that there has been no excess cash flow and that all assets have been accumulated by borrowing. It also means that this person or couple is bankrupt—they could not meet their debts even if they sold everything.

The propensity to borrow is a ratio that I use in financial analysis, merely to point out that accumulation of things is not the objective. Accumulation can be done through borrowed funds, and it does not mean that just because there are many things accumulated, one has a secure financial situation. Debt against those things means that in reality they are not owned by the one who has them, but rather by the lender. Proverbs 22:7 says ". . . the borrower is servant to the lender."

Propensity to Accumulate

Another measurement necessary in doing a financial analysis is the propensity to accumulate, which is calculated by dividing net worth by the number of years worked. It is merely an indicator of how much accumulation on the average has taken place each year and also indicates where that couple might end up financially if they continued at that rate of accumulation.

For example, Bob and Laura's net worth of $36,000 divided by 20, the number of years that Bob has worked, means that they have been able to accumulate, on the average, $1,800 per year. If Bob still has thirty years of productivity left, and continues to accumulate at $1,800 per year, he will end up at retirement with a net worth of $54,000. However, if that amount of $1,800 can be compounded at a reasonable investment rate, they will have accumulated substantially more than $54,000. We will look at the magic of compounding in Week Five. For now, we know they are making progress toward the accomplishment of their long-term goals, but they can be much more strategic in accomplishing those goals with sound financial planning.

There is no right level for the propensity to accumulate because it depends upon the long-term goals, but the higher it is, the sooner you will achieve your long-term goals. Determining the propensity to borrow and the propensity to accumulate points out that the higher the debt ratio or propensity to borrow, the lower the propensity to accumulate. Simply stated, borrowing does not always help you to achieve your financial goals and objectives.

During the very first seminar on financial planning that I taught, an older couple was preparing their statement of net worth. I heard the wife say to the husband, "I didn't know we owned that," and a little bit later, "When did we buy that?" and somewhat later, "Why do we have that debt?" In talking with them later, I learned that the two of them had never prepared a statement of net worth together, and only the husband knew approximately where they stood financially. I have subsequently found that this is very common—that a husband and wife rarely sit down and discuss where they are financially by looking at an actual statement of their net worth. To get and stay on track for financial security, I've found it is absolutely critical for a couple or individual to prepare and review a statement of net worth *annually*.

Referring back to your Inventory of Assets and Liabilities, complete your Personal Balance Sheet.

A Review of Bob and Laura's Personal Balance Sheet

1. **NET WORTH**
   Assets:

Liquid	$	9,000
Nonliquid		146,000
Total:	$	155,000
Less: Total Liabilities:		(119,000)
Net Worth:	$	36,000

2. **LIQUIDITY** $ 9,000
   For emergencies, bills, major purchases &
   investment opportunities

3. **PRODUCTIVE ASSETS** $ 24,000
   (Liabilities divided by assets)
   Generating or having the potential to generate
   income

Liquid Assets	$ 9,000
Real Estate	$15,000

4. PROPENSITY TO BORROW   _____ 77%
   (Liabilities divided by assets) × 100
          $119,000
          $155,000

5. PROPENSITY TO ACCUMULATE $_____ 1,800/year
   (Net worth divided by years worked)
          $36,000
          20 years

Your Personal Balance Sheet

1. NET WORTH
   Assets:
        Liquid $_____
        Nonliquid   _____
   Total: $_____
   Less: Total Liabilities: (_____)
   Net Worth: $_____

2. LIQUIDITY $_____
   (for emergencies, bills, major purchases &
   investment opportunities)

3. PRODUCTIVE ASSETS $_____
   (Liabilities divided by assets)

4. PROPENSITY TO BORROW   _____ %
   (Liabilities divided by assets) × 100

5. PROPENSITY TO ACCUMULATE $_____
   (Net worth divided by years worked)

WHAT YOUR PERSONAL BALANCE SHEET TELLS YOU

You've now determined your net worth, your propensity to borrow, and your propensity to accumulate. You now know more about your financial situation than the great majority of Americans—you are on your way to sound financial footing.

However, Laura's frustration when she asked, "How can we make so much money and never have any?" is not at all uncommon. Like Bob and Laura, most couples have short-term commitments and priorities that frequently have them spending more than they earn or that mandate that both spouses work. Although you won't be preparing a cash-flow summary until next week, preparing your statement of net worth may have indicated a relatively high propensity to borrow. That tells you, as you may have already realized, that you perhaps—and even probably—are funding an annual negative cash flow margin with increased credit card use or consumer debt. One of the goals of the financial planning process is to develop a cash flow margin, meaning taking the action necessary to spend less than you earn. In order to achieve your long-term goals, you must have a positive cash flow margin.

Look again at our Financial Planning Diagram on page 33 and observe that, first of all, the long-term goals will probably require substantial financial resources, and second, without receiving either an inheritance or striking oil, the only way to reach your long-term goals is to spend less than you earn over time.

This is the hard part, because in order to generate enough cash-flow margin each year to meet your long-term goals, you have to make the long term a priority over the short term. A friend of mine once defined financial maturity as "being able to give up today's desires for future benefits." If I choose to give up something today in order to accumulate or save for tomorrow, I have probably made a wise financial decision. But the question is, where do you cut? The tithe should not be cut (although this is the first to go for many Christian couples when finances get tight); taxes cannot be cut without either reducing your income or spending cash on some deductible item; debt repayment cannot and should not be cut. The only area left is your lifestyle. However, many lifestyle expenses cannot be easily cut because of previous commitments such as where you live, how many mouths you have to feed, and so on. Outside influences from a worldly point of view—advertisers, friends, neighbors, other Christians, and even Christian leaders—may lead you to believe that you are entitled to or have a right to a lifestyle that may very well be beyond what you can afford.

You can easily determine what the appropriate lifestyle for you should be, based on your present income and commitments, by working through this planning worksheet:

Amount Available for Lifestyle

Total Income	$_____
Less: Tithe	(_____)
Less: Taxes (all)	(_____)
Less: Debt repayment	(_____)
Less: Savings for long-term	(_____)
Balance	$_____

The balance is the amount available for the funding of your lifestyle. Granted, this may seem simplistic, but God's answers don't have to be difficult. In completing this worksheet, you need to acknowledge that:

- You may not achieve the lifestyle level you are seeking immediately;
- Your tithe is just the beginning of giving;
- Planning can affect the amount paid in taxes;
- God may choose to increase your income.

But to presume any of these things will happen is a violation of a biblical directive.

> Come now, you who say, "Today or tomorrow we will go to such and such a city, spend a year there, buy and sell, and make a profit"; whereas you do not know what will happen tomorrow. For what is your life? It is even a vapor that appears for a little time and then vanishes away. Instead you ought to say, "If the Lord wills, we shall live and do this or that." But now you boast in your arrogance. All such boasting is evil. Therefore, to him who knows to do good and does not do it, to him it is sin.
>
> —James 4:13–17

The point of this lifestyle worksheet is that you must plan to have a cash flow margin if you are going to achieve your long-term goals—*it will not happen without planning*—and the only truly discretionary place to cut spending, in order to generate this margin, is in the area of lifestyle. However, to do so will be very, very, very difficult. Very few people, Christians or non-Christians, will be supportive. Frankly, you will be able to change your life-style only by the grace of God. But with God, nothing is impossible. Perhaps you've heard the saying, "Trust God, but keep rowing to shore." Trust God with your resources, and continue to do your financial planning. Through this process, you will learn the tools and techniques to reduce living expenses, get out of debt, and stay out of debt. Stick with your commitment to financial planning and you *will* see results!

IN PREPARATION FOR YOUR NEXT SESSION

Because of the critical importance of understanding the economic and spiritual implications of debt, and the detailed work necessary in compiling your cash flow summary, next week's session may well be the most lengthy in developing your plan. You might want to read the material on debt before your scheduled weekly session; then you will not feel rushed as you use the scheduled time to work through the cash-flow analysis.

Where Does All the Money Go?

Confronting the Dangers of Debt

If your statement of net worth can be compared to a snapshot or an X-ray, then the summary of your cash flow can be likened to a movie. Cash flow is not a static measurement at a point in time like a net worth statement, but is rather a dynamic measurement of cash inflows and cash outflows over a defined period. Cash flow is either retrospective, a summary of what has happened over a period of time in the past, or it is prospective, a projection of what is going to happen over a period of time in the future.

If you look again at the Financial-Planning Diagram, you will notice that there are six elements to cash flow. First there is the inflow, which comes from salary, business income, earnings or investments, and pension retirement income. Then there are five outflows: giving, taxes, debt repayment, living expenses, and accumulation.

After completing your Personal Balance Sheet, you now have a clear picture of your indebtedness and your track record in accumulation. Although there is no "right" level for accumulation, the probability is that you are far more likely to borrow than accumulate. As we said in the second chapter, 80 percent of Americans owe more than they own. What you now need to examine in order to answer the question Where am I? is exactly where all your income goes.

This week you will analyze your living expenses in totality by completing a detailed cash-flow summary. However, in our society, living expenses, lifestyle, and debt are inextricably intertwined. Analyzing where your cash flow goes *must* be done in the context of first looking at the economic and spiritual dangers of debt.

I want to remind you that when you've finished this session, *we are still not ready to look at solutions*. Again, be patient and trust the process. God is in control of your past, your present, and your future. By committing to this process of financial planning, you are being faithful—let God take care of the results. Before examining your income, giving, taxes, indebtedness, and living expenses, we need to look at the issue of debt.

THE DANGERS OF DEBT

The financial area of debt is clouded with more emotion, misunderstanding, and poor teaching than any other area. Let's clarify a basic biblical truth regarding debt and understanding what debt is and is not:

- Debt is not a sin. The Bible discourages the use of debt, but does not prohibit it.
- Debt can be defined many ways. I define it as "any money owed to anyone for anything."

There are five different kinds of debt:

1. Credit card debt;
2. Consumer debt;
3. Mortgage debt;
4. Investment debt;
5. Business debt.

Getting in debt is as easy as getting down an ice-covered mountain. Getting out of debt is just as difficult as climbing that same mountain. Debt becomes a trap, mortgaging the future, with both economic and spiritual dangers. In many cases, borrowing money can be no more difficult than signing your name or, at the most, filling out a lengthy form. Even borrowing the initial money for investments or starting a business can be almost effortless. It's so easy; getting in takes no effort, but getting out can be next to impossible.

Borrowing money, for whatever reason, gives a great feeling of satisfaction and power—initially. However, indebtedness always carries a hidden trap, one which is realized when the borrowed money must be paid back. By that time, the glamour has worn off whatever was purchased and the money used to repay the debt takes away the opportunity to buy other things. For example, assume that a couple overspends their income $1,000 each year for ten years on impulsive purchases, a surprisingly easy thing to do. *Only $2.74 a day spent on impulse items will result in an expenditure of $1,000 per year on completely nonproductive purchases!* Then realizing that they are $10,000 in debt, they decide to begin a program to get out of debt. By this point, not only are they overspending by $1,000 each year, but they are also paying at least $1,000 per year in interest (if the interest rate is only 10 percent). Consider the ease of debt growth by reviewing the following chart:

Ease of Debt Growth

	Overspending	Total Debt	Interest Paid
Year 1	$ 1,000	$ 1,000	$ 100
Year 2	1,000	2,000	200
Year 3	1,000	3,000	300
Year 4	1,000	4,000	400
Year 5	1,000	5,000	500
Year 6	1,000	6,000	600
Year 7	1,000	7,000	700
Year 8	1,000	8,000	800
Year 9	1,000	9,000	900
Year 10	1,000	10,000	1,000
Total	$10,000		$5,500

When this couple decides to get out of debt, first of all they must stop going into debt. Second, they must begin to pay back the accumulated debt, and all the while, continue to pay the interest. Their real costs are shown in the True Cost of Debt chart on pages 53–54.

Debt Repayment

	Debt Repayment	Total Debt	Interest Paid
Year 11	$ 1,000	$ 9,000	$1,000
Year 12	1,000	8,000	900
Year 13	1,000	7,000	800
Year 14	1,000	6,000	700
Year 15	1,000	5,000	600
Year 16	1,000	4,000	500
Year 17	1,000	3,000	400
Year 18	1,000	2,000	300
Year 19	1,000	1,000	200
Year 20	1,000	-0-	100
Total	**$10,000**		$5,500

True Cost of Debt

	Overspending Reduction	Debt Repayment	Interest Paid	Total Cost
Year 1	$ 0	$ 0	$ 100	$ 100
Year 2	0	0	200	200
Year 3	0	0	300	300
Year 4	0	0	400	400
Year 5	0	0	500	500
Year 6	0	0	600	600
Year 7	0	0	700	700
Year 8	0	0	800	800
Year 9	0	0	900	900
Year 10	0	0	1,000	1,000
Year 11	1,000	1,000	1,000	3,000
Year 12	1,000	1,000	900	2,900
Year 13	1,000	1,000	800	2,800
Year 14	1,000	1,000	700	2,700
Year 15	1,000	1,000	600	2,600
Year 16	1,000	1,000	500	2,500
Year 17	1,000	1,000	400	2,400
Year 18	1,000	1,000	300	2,300

	Overspending Reduction	Debt Repayment	Interest Paid	Total Cost
Year 19	$ 1,000	$ 1,000	$ 200	$ 2,200
Year 20	1,000	1,000	100	2,100
Total	$10,000	$10,000	$11,000	$31,000

Their actual cost of overspending by $10,000 ($1,000 per year for ten years) is $31,000. Notice that when they made their decision to get out of debt in year ten, their only cost was $1,000 per year in interest, but immediately after their decision in year eleven, the effective cost went to $3,000, because they must forego in years eleven through twenty the overspending formerly done in years one through ten. Just think—$21,000 that could have been used in far more productive and fun ways!

There is another hidden cost of their indebtedness: the income-tax consequences. In year eleven, not only must they earn the $3,000 cost, but they must also earn the taxes on that $3,000 in order to have $3,000 left to pay the lender. They must earn $4,000 in order to have $3,000 left.

Income	$4,000
Taxes at 25%	1,000
Balance available	$3,000

The Bottom Line of Debt

The bottom line, economically, to the danger of debt is this: Debt always mortgages the future. The first-priority use of future income must be debt repayment—not giving or lifestyle or investing or even taxes! The freedom of choice disappears.

The consequences of debt are a paradox. Current marketplace wisdom says to you, "Raise your standard of living by buying what you want now, and pay for it while you enjoy it," but the reality is that you are probably sentencing yourself to a lower standard of living in the future. Look again at the True Cost of Debt Chart on pages 53–54.

This couple enjoyed themselves to the tune of $1,000 per year beyond their income in the first ten years, but their second ten years was being mortgaged and resulted in a much greater cost than the earlier benefit. The paradox is that while apparently raising their standard of living, they were in reality, over the long term lowering it. What a deception! This illustration may portray why so many couples go through some very difficult times or divorce after eight to twelve years of marriage.

The Spiritual Dangers of Debt

Over the years I have started several businesses of my own and have had the privilege of counseling many hundreds of others who have been in the initial stages of founding their own businesses. One of the things that is standard in starting a business is to secure from a bank a line of credit or some terms of financing so there is always cash available to meet the unexpected needs of a new business. Therefore, when I started this business in the fall of 1979, I went to the bank and arranged for a line of credit.

In the following weeks, as I prayed through the many issues regarding the starting of this business, I felt less and less comfortable with having borrowed to start my business, even though it made "good business sense." Eventually, I felt so strongly convicted about the need not to have debt that I called the bank and canceled my line of credit. This was an extremely risky thing to do, as I had a totally unproven business, no clients, and very little financial resources personally.

Approximately one week after I canceled the line of credit, I was visiting in the training department of a major international corporation headquartered in Atlanta. During the conversation with one of the training directors, he asked me if I had any interest in developing a financial-planning seminar for his organization. As a matter of fact, I had been in the process at that very time of developing a financial-planning seminar in order to provide a conceptual framework for the financial-planning process. Of course, I said yes. He then asked me how much I would charge them to develop such a seminar. I had no idea what large corporations paid for such work, so I simply asked, "What would you pay?"

He thought for a moment before saying they would pay me $6,000 to develop the seminar and another $4,000 if I would teach it four times during the next year—a total of $10,000. Coincidentally, the line of credit I had arranged at the bank was for $10,000. Of course, I replied that $10,000 for that work sounded "very fair." He also asked me if they could go ahead and pay me the $6,000 immediately in order to get it into the current year's budget. With no hesitation I gave him my address.

In many cases, when we borrow the money to fund an item, for the purpose of a new car, a television, a new home, a vacation, or whatever, we are putting the lender in the place of God. Who needs God to provide for us if someone will lend to us?

The spiritual dangers of borrowing money are twofold: (1) Borrowing *always* presumes upon the future; (2) borrowing *may* deny God an opportunity to work.

The Bible definitely warns us about presuming upon the future. Again, I'll refer to James 4:13–17: "Come now, you who say, 'Today or tomorrow we will go to such and such a city, spend a year there, buy and sell, and make a profit'; whereas you do not know what will happen tomorrow. For what is your life? It is even a vapor that appears for a little time and then vanishes away. Instead you ought to say, 'If the Lord wills, we shall live and do this or that.' But now you boast in your arrogance. All such boasting is evil. Therefore, to him who knows to do good and does not do it, to him it is sin." James clearly tell us that presuming upon the future is "arrogance." In Luke 14:28, Jesus said: "For which of you, intending to build a tower, does not sit down first and count the cost, whether he has enough to finish it?" Whenever any money is borrowed for any purpose, there is a presumption of repayment. In fact, from the lender's viewpoint it is not only a presumption, it is a certainty. Psalm 37:21 says in part, "The wicked borrows and does not repay."

The biblical principle that flows out of that truth is this:

Whenever you borrow money for any reason, there must be a *guaranteed* way to pay it back.

Not a "hoped-for" way, such as an increase in income nor even the continuation of income, but a guaranteed way *regardless* of circumstances. If this principle were followed, there would be almost no risk to debt. Not to have a guaranteed way to repay is *always* to presume upon the future.

I am convinced that had I not canceled the line of credit with the bank and depended solely upon God to provide the resources, I never would have received the contract to design the seminar. I am convinced that had I borrowed the money, the training director would never have made the offer he did, because to this day I can take no credit for having received the money. God provided it in an unusual, undeniable, and supernatural fashion.

We seem to be unwilling to wait for God's timing and for God's method to meet our needs and our desires. We prefer to have it done our way on our timing. Yet Isaiah 55:8–9 says, " 'For My thoughts are not your thoughts, / Nor are your ways My ways,' says the LORD. 'For as the heavens are higher than the earth, / So are My ways higher than your ways, / And My thoughts than your thoughts.' " Invariably, God's method of meeting my needs and desires is different from my method. The question that we need to ask ourselves is, "Does God provide for what I want by providing borrowed funds, or is this *me* meeting my needs and desires in my *own* way?"

BIBLICAL PRINCIPLES OF BORROWING

The Bible contains many passages dealing with money and specifically debt. In addition to presuming upon the future and potentially denying God an opportunity to work, there are many other biblical principles relative to debt and borrowing. In reading the Bible, we need to ask ourselves, "Why is so much written about debt in God's Word?" Both as a Christian and a financial planner, I believe there are three reasons.

First, debt is extremely deceptive. As we observed earlier, getting into debt is extremely easy—getting out is next to impossible.

Second, debt creates bondage, and if that bondage is to the world system, we are no longer free to be the witnesses in this world that God has called us to be.

Third, debt is almost blasphemous when by using it we deny God an opportunity to work.

I encourage you to look at the following key scriptures and ask yourself, "What is God telling me about debt through this verse?" Record your thoughts in the spaces provided.

The wicked borrows and does not repay,
But the righteous shows mercy and gives.

—Psalm 37:21

_____

_____

_____

Owe no one anything except to love one another, for he who loves another has fulfilled the law.

—Romans 13:8

_____

_____

_____

The rich rules over the poor,
And the borrower is servant to the lender.

—Proverbs 22:7

_____

_____

_____

But if anyone does not provide for his own, and especially for those of his household, he has denied the faith and is worse than an unbeliever.
—1 Timothy 5:8

_____

_____

_____

Take heed and beware of covetousness, for one's life does not consist in the abundance of the things he possesses.

—Luke 12:15

_____

_____

_____

Although the context of the passage from Romans does not deal specifically with finances (and even if it did, I do not believe it prohibits debt), it does say, "If I owe anyone anything, I am not free to give love to that person." Anyone who has borrowed money from another person, and especially another Christian, realizes the wall that immediately goes up from being in a debtor/lender relationship. The reality is that whenever you have borrowed from anyone, you are a servant to that person.

However, with all these cautions against debt, I still believe that in some cases debt is acceptable, but only under certain conditions.

Four Criteria for Undertaking Any Debt

Criteria #1: Does it make economic sense?

Rule to follow:
- The cost to borrow (after-tax interest) must be less than the economic benefit received (interest, yield, and/or growth in value).
- There must be a *guaranteed* way of repayment.

Criteria #2: Are both spouses free from any anxiety regarding this debt?

Rule to follow:
- There must be unity between spouses.

Criteria #3: Can the debt be undertaken with spiritual peace of mind?

Rule to follow:
- If I experience any lack of peace when I picture myself taking on this debt, I do not enter into the debt.

Criteria #4: What personal goals and values am I meeting with this debt that can be met no *other way?*

Rule to follow:
- Ask myself if I am funding my *needs* or my *greed*. In other words, is this something I *want* or something I really *need?*

These four criteria are practical, biblical, and pragmatic and should be applied, emotions aside, to every debt opportunity. Applying these criteria to the five kinds of debt, we can draw the following conclusions.

Credit Card Debt. It will never satisfy the economic criteria and, therefore, should never be used. Using credit cards, which always have a high interest rate, to accumulate consumptive and depreciating items makes no sense economically. Whether or not to use credit cards for convenience will be addressed in Week Seven.

Consumer Debt. Consumer debt is debt used to finance cars, furniture, vacations, and other consumptive and depreciating items. It is exactly like credit card debt except that the process of applying for it is usually more lengthy. Because it is just like credit card debt, it should be avoided at all costs.

Both credit card and consumer debt are to be avoided, not because they are sinful, but because they just don't make sense economically. The only exception (and I have never seen an example of this) would be using them for a personal goal and value that could be met in no other way, a personal goal and value that unquestionably came from God. Implicitly, this says that God has chosen debt to meet a personal need. Again, I have never seen an example of this, but I would not want to put God into a box and say that He could never do it.

Mortgage Debt. We Americans have come to believe that owning a home is a God-given right. We have trained our children to expect to begin their married lives in a home it took our parents a lifetime to save for! Additionally, during the last thirty-five to forty years, and especially the years 1960 to 1980, a home purchased with a fixed interest rate was the safest and surest way to build personal net worth and equity. Beginning in 1983, however, the "rules of the game" changed; inflation slowed down and deflation has occurred in some parts of the country. Additionally, interest rates have proven to be much more volatile in the last ten years. It has taken a while for our society to recognize this, and I don't believe we have, as yet, accepted the consequences of those changes.

When considering the purchase of a home, we should apply the same four criteria for undertaking any debt. However, the economic criteria are very difficult to nail down in today's economic environment. Even in the period 1960 to 1980, there was not a guaranteed way to pay the debt except for returning the home back to the lending institution. My counsel to young couples who are considering the purchase of a home is never to become so attached to the home that they could not give it up if the debt could not be paid. Jobs are not nearly as secure today as they were in the past. Inflation and fixed low-interest rates are certainly not sure things.

The psychological burden of a home-mortgage debt is more severe than most people think. Studies have shown that having mortgage debt is a stressful factor and that the degree of stress relates to the amount of mortgage.[1]

The question of whether or not to pay off the mortgage, if that is an option, is really an economic, psychological, and spiritual decision. Economi-

---

[1]Psychiatrist Thomas H. Holmes and his colleagues at the University of Washington School of Medicine have developed a scale to measure the relative stress induced by various changes in a person's life. The amount of stress is measured on a point scale of 200 "life-change units." A mortgage over $10,000 is one of the stress inducing events identified in the studies, placing in the top twenty of forty-two changes or events. For a more detailed look at the "Vulnerability of Stress Scale," please refer to page 66 in the revised hardback edition of *Master Your Money* by Ron Blue, Thomas Nelson Publishers, © 1991.

cally, it may not make sense to pay off a low-interest-rate mortgage, even if one has the funds to do so. However, psychologically and spiritually, it may be the best course. Remember, finances are nothing more than a resource to accomplish other goals and objectives—they are never an end in themselves. Therefore, even if it does not make economic sense to pay off a mortgage, there may be higher priority goals and objectives that need to be met. Money then becomes merely the resource to meet those goals. The decision does not have to be always an economic one. That counsel is, of course, good for all decisions.

Investment and Business Debt. Applying the four basic criteria for any debt is a good idea before taking on investment or business debt. Let's review the four criteria:

1. Is the rate of return greater than the cost, both on an after-tax basis?
2. Is there a guaranteed way to repay the debt?
3. Are both spouses in perfect agreement and unity?
4. Do you have spiritual peace of mind when considering this debt?

I probably see a thousand "good deals" cross my desk each year. My experience has been that no business opportunity or investment opportunity ever comes packaged as anything other than "a good deal." No one has ever come to my office or sent a proposal and said, "Let me show you a bad deal." On the front end, every business and investment deal is a good one. It only goes bad later. What makes investment and business debts so difficult to evaluate and reject is that they are all presented as good deals, deals which a person would be foolish to turn down. Therefore, there never seems to be economic justification alone for turning them down.

This is one of the reasons why I feel it is so important to apply the rule that spouses have perfect unity on their debt decisions. I remember speaking one time to a group of professional athletes, and as I related that rule with them, one of the wives sat with tears streaming down her cheeks. Afterward she shared with me how her husband, who had played on three Super Bowl championship teams, had been presented with a business opportunity that was a "sure thing." Against his wife's counsel, he had mortgaged everything, gone into the business and eventually lost all they owned. What does a forty-year-old former athlete with no training or money and a family do? It was a tragic, yet typical, case.

When considering business opportunities these recommendations may save you years of heartache and regret: First, if you cannot explain the deal or investment to your spouse in such a way that he or she totally understands it, don't do it. Second, even if you can explain it so that your spouse totally understands it, but he or she feels uneasy or unsure in any way about it, don't do it.

Granted, you may pass up many opportunities. However, one of the surest ways to financial success is to avoid the major mistakes (which we will address in Week Five), because not only do you have to make up for the lost investment, but you also lose the earnings that this money could have generated, and the earnings that the earnings could have generated, and the earnings that the earnings that the earnings could have generated. Again, the biblical counsel is sound: "He who gathers money little by little makes it grow." The best way to get rich is to get rich slowly.

Please understand that I am not being judgmental, because I know better than most the temptation that debt presents. Again, let me emphasize that debt is not sin. The Bible discourages the use of debt, but does not prohibit it. Being in debt is never the real problem; rather it is only symptomatic of the real problem. My book entitled *The Debt Squeeze* details more of what I've learned on this difficult issue.

However, if you—like many Americans—find the bills pile higher, the debt grows deeper, and the anxiety increases each month, *take heart*. You are addressing your situation in a responsible faithful manner by working through this financial-planning process. The question you need to consider at this point is not, "How do we get out of debt?" The real question to ask yourself as you analyze your cash flow is, "Why am I in this situation?" Quite possibly core issues such as compulsive spending, low self-esteem, fears, insecurities, or greed are fueling your indebtedness.[2]

Without dwelling on the past, or limiting God's power in the future, with radical honesty, consider the question, *Why am I (we) in this situation?* Record your reflections here, and if you are working through this financial

---

[2]If your financial situation is causing you significant emotional or relational distress (for example, chronic insomnia, frequent marital disputes, or anxiety attacks) I strongly encourage you to seek professional counsel. God will be faithful if you seek His healing; however, addressing these core issues is beyond the scope of this financial-planning process.

plan with your spouse, share your thoughts with each other. Then place your total indebtedness in God's hands. You may want to use the simple prayer of surrender offered below.

Asking the Tough Question

Why am I (we) in debt to this extent?_____

_____

_____

_____

_____

_____

Surrendering the Debt Despair

God, we have gotten deeper in debt than we ever anticipated or intended. We know that in so doing, we have not been wise stewards of Your resources, and may have to make some radical changes in our lifestyle. We ask for the courage to be honest with ourselves, the strength to be faithful to Your principles, the creativity to be resourceful, and the guidance to know what actions to take. In Your Spirit and by Your grace we surrender our financial situation to You. In Jesus' name. Amen.

Trust in the LORD with all your heart,
And lean not on your own understanding;
In all your ways acknowledge Him,
And He shall direct your paths.

                                            —Proverbs 3:5–6

DETERMINING YOUR CASH FLOW

Review again the Financial-Planning Diagram on page 33 and notice that there are six elements to cash flow. First there is inflow, which comes from salary, business income, earnings or investments, and pension retirement income; and then there are five outflows: giving, taxes, debt repayment, living expenses, and accumulation. We will examine the cash flow for Bob and Laura in five steps:

1. Projecting their income in Exhibit A (see page 66).
2. Projecting their giving for the next twelve months in Exhibit B (see page 67).
3. Projecting their tax liabilities in Exhibit C (see page 67).
4. Projecting their debt repayment in Exhibit D (see page 68).
5. Projecting their living expenses over the next twelve months in Exhibit E (see page 68).

Once these steps have been taken, we will analyze the results by listing each of these areas in a cash-flow summary to determine your cash-flow margin. Before tackling your worksheets, you will find it helpful to first review Bob and Laura's situation. Their projected income (Exhibit A) over the next twelve months is $3,750 per month from salaries and then $4,600, which is not received on a monthly basis, for a total annual amount of $49,600, which by itself looks pretty good. However, this is without considering the outflow.

You should also note that it was necessary to prepare the statement of net worth *first* in order not to miss the income from such things as interest on the savings account and the real estate investment, which generates a cash flow of $2,000 per year. In addition to salaries and wages, dividends, interest, etc., there may be sales of assets, pension plan liquidations, and commissions. (Commissions are difficult to project because they are unknown. I recommend that you project commission income on a conservative basis as you estimate a projected cash flow.)

Giving. The giving amounts from Exhibit B are again of two types: those that are given on a monthly basis, and those that are given on some other basis, such as annually, as a result of an appeal or pledge that has been made previously. The total indicates that Bob and Laura are projecting to give $2,200 for the next year.

Taxes. The tax summary that is projected for Bob and Laura includes all income taxes and Social Security taxes, but not property taxes or other types of taxes. The information with which to prepare this summary came from their pay stubs. In addition to the deductions and withholding, a person might be subject to tax estimates, which are paid on a quarterly basis. In Bob and Laura's case, they are paying a total of $835 per month of tax withholdings or $10,014 on an annual basis.

Debt Repayment. Exhibit D, the Debt Repayment Schedule, is the same schedule as prepared for the liability section of the net worth statement (see page 40) with the exception that the mortgage loan amount has been left out and is not included in the total. The mortgage loan payment is included in the living expenses section in Exhibit E. In some cases no payment is being made or is intended to be made and therefore it is not included in the payment schedule. For example, the loan from the parents—there is no intention on Bob and Laura's part of repaying that loan. (Parents, beware!) Additionally, the life insurance loan will not be repaid; therefore it shows no payment. Bob and Laura are paying $713 per month in debt repayment. The annual amount, then, is $8,556.

Living Expenses. Exhibit E, the living expense schedule for Bob and Laura, shows monthly expenses of $2,037 for the twelve-month period. Expenses paid other than monthly are $11,050 for a total annual living expense of $35,594.

Their mortgage payment is included under housing expenses, while the car payment is not included under transportation. The car payment is listed under the Debt Repayment Schedule, Exhibit D. (Car payments are generally considered a more discretionary type of expense.) In every case, Bob and Laura estimated their expenses and for the monthly amounts, they estimated average expenses.

Cash-Flow Margin. Bob and Laura can now summarize each of the exhibits into a Cash Flow Analysis as illustrated on page 71. Two primary observations emerge from this summary. First of all, the cash-flow margin after all living expenses are subtracted from the gross income is a negative $6,664. This means that with no further planning on their part, they will have to do one of four things:

1. Increase their income
2. Reduce their expenses
3. Dip into their savings
4. Borrow additional monies in order not to have a negative cash flow for the year

Since Bob and Laura are typical, chances are pretty good that they did not even know they were running a cash flow margin that was negative. It probably crept up on them month-by-month. They also probably increased their credit card debt, considered a consolidation loan, or Laura may have considered working outside the home. Now that the problem has been defined, the solution is much easier to determine.

Net Spendable Income. In addition to the cash flow margin, this summary uses the concept of Net Spendable Income. The Net Spendable Income basically says that the first three priority uses of money are giving, taxes, and debt repayment. The amount of spendable income, then, is the amount left. The net spendable income concept establishes the priorities of income and says that living expenses should be the fourth priority, as opposed to typically being the first.

As we've already established, giving should be proportionate and should come out of the firstfruits (1 Cor. 16:2; Prov. 3:9). Taxes are an obligation to the believer and therefore a priority (Rom. 13:7). Debt repayment is a must for the believer (Ps. 37:21). If Scripture gives us these three priorities, then living expenses are discretionary, manageable, and a fourth priority, biblically.

Bob & Laura's Projected Income

Exhibit A

	AMOUNT PAID MONTHLY	AMOUNT PAID ANNUALLY	TOTAL ANNUAL AMOUNT
SOURCES:			
Gross wages: husband	$3,750		$45,000
Gross wages: wife		2,550	2,550
Dividends			
Dividends			
Dividends			
Interest: savings		50	50
Interest			
Rents (cash flow)			
Business			
Pensions & annuities			
Other: real estate		2,000	2,000

	AMOUNT PAID MONTHLY	AMOUNT PAID ANNUALLY	TOTAL ANNUAL AMOUNT
Other			
Other			
Total gross income	$3,750	$4,600	$49,600

Bob & Laura's Projected Giving

Exhibit B

ORGANIZATION	MONTHLY	ANNUAL	TOTAL
Church	50		600
Other: Christian Ministry A	20		240
Other: Christian Ministry B		400	400
Other: Fishing Federation	80		960
Other			
Other			
Other			
Other			
Other			
TOTAL	$150	$400	$2,200

Bob & Laura's Tax Summary

Exhibit C

DEDUCTIONS AND WITHHOLDINGS	MONTHLY	ANNUAL	TOTAL ANNUAL
Federal income tax	410	0	4,920
State & city income tax	138	0	1,650
Social Security	287	0	3,444
Total Tax	$835	$0	$10,014

Bob & Laura's Debt Repayment

Exhibit D

Creditor	Balance Due	Interest Rate	Payment Schedule Per month	Until when
1. Charge cards	$ 3,000	18%	$ 50	Forever
2. Auto loans	6,000	12%	263	3 yrs
3. Parents	5,000	6%	—	?
4. Boat loan	5,000	14%	200	3 yrs
5. Bank loan	13,500	15%	200	10 yrs
6. Life insurance	5,000	5%	—	?
7.				
8.				
9.				
10.				
Totals	**$37,500**		**$713**	

Bob & Laura's Living Expenses

Exhibit E

YEAR: Current	Amount Paid Monthly	Amount Paid Other Than Monthly	Total Annual Amount
HOUSING			
Mortgage/rent	$ 684		$ 8,208
Insurance		400	400
Property taxes		1,000	1,000
Electricity	60		720
Heating	40		480
Water	30		360
Sanitation			
Telephone	40		480
Cleaning			
Repairs/maintenance	20		240

YEAR: Current	Amount Paid Monthly	Amount Paid Other Than Monthly	Total Annual Amount
Improvements			
Furnishings	50		600
Supplies	10		120
Other			
Total Housing	934	1,400	12,608
FOOD	400		4,800
CLOTHING			
Husband		250	250
Wife		250	250
Children		500	500
Total Clothing		1,000	1,000
TRANSPORTATION			
Insurance		500	500
Gas & oil	150		1,800
Repairs/maintenance	30		360
Parking			
Mass transit or commute			
Other			
Total Transportation	180	500	2,660
ENTERTAINMENT/RECREATION			
Eating out	40		480
Babysitters	10		120
Magazines/newspapers/cable	20		240
Vacation		1,000	1,000
Clubs/activities		300	300
Classes/courses			
Other			
Total Entertainment	70	1,300	2,140

MEDICAL EXPENSES

Insurance	60		720
Doctors	20		240
Dentists	20		240
Drugs	5		60
Total Medical Expenses	105		1,260

INSURANCE

Life	128		1,536
Disability			
Other			
Total Insurance	128		1,536

CHILDREN

School Lunches	30		360
Allowances	20		240
Tuition		6,000	6,000
Lessons	20		240
Other	10		120
Total Children	80	6,000	6,960

GIFTS/SPECIAL OCCASIONS

Christmas		500	500
Birthdays		150	150
Anniversary		200	200
Holidays other than Christmas			300
Other	25		25
Total Gifts	25	850	1,150

MISCELLANEOUS

Toiletries	25		300
Husband: lunches, etc.	20		240
Wife: miscellaneous	20		240
Dry cleaning/laundry	20		240

Animal care: license, food, vet	10		120
Beauty/barber	20		240
Other			
Other			
Total Miscellaneous	115		1,380
TOTAL LIVING EXPENSES	**$2,037**	**$11,050**	**$35,494**

Bob & Laura's Cash Flow Analysis

GROSS INCOME (Exhibit A page 66)		$49,600
LESS:		
Giving (Exhibit B page 67)	$ 2,200	
Taxes (Exhibit C page 67)	10,014	
Debt (Exhibit D page 68)	8,556	
Total Expenses		(20,770)
Net Spendable Income		$28,830
(Gross Income Less Expenses)		
Living Expenses (Exhibit E pages 68–71)		
Housing	12,608	
Food	4,800	
Clothing	1,000	
Transportation	2,660	
Entertainment/recreation	2,140	
Medical	1,260	
Insurance	1,536	
Children	6,960	
Gifts	1,150	
Miscellaneous	1,380	
Total Living Expenses		(35,594)
Cash Flow Margin		$(6,664)
(Net Spendable Less Living Expenses)		

EXISTING MARGIN COMMITMENTS:

_____   _____

_____   _____

_____   _____

Total Commitments   _____

UNCOMMITTED MARGIN $_____

FINDING OUT WHERE IT ALL GOES

Remember you are not yet ready to work on solutions. You are still in the process of determining where you are. Using the charts on pages 66 through 71, prepare your own cash flow summary. The following guidelines may be helpful.

Exhibit A: Your Projected Income

1. Calculate your monthly income from salary and wages for both husband and wife. Note that the amounts should be GROSS income (before taxes and other deductions). To determine monthly amounts:
    - If you are paid on a weekly basis, use one week's pay multiplied by 4.3 (weeks per month).
    - If you are paid every two weeks, i.e., you get 26 paychecks per year, multiply your two-week paycheck by 2.17. This will compensate for the two months of the year in which you will receive three paychecks.
    - If the checks are not always the same due to irregular hours (overtime, shift differential, etc.), then use an average pay per month as the salary.
    - If your pay is on a commission-only basis, then use an average of the past few years or what you consider a reasonable income projection. As I said earlier, be conservative!

2. Dividends and interest should be projected annually unless these funds are being used on a monthly basis.

3. Rents you receive should be shown as "net rents." Example: Rental income

is $7,200 per year. You pay $5,400 on the mortgage, $200 for repairs and $500 in taxes. The net rent is $1,100.

4. Include income from all other sources such as in-home babysitting, hobbies, crafts, gifts, etc.

5. Business income would include income from self-employment, freelance work, income-producing hobbies, or other business interests.

Your Projected Income

	AMOUNT PAID MONTHLY	AMOUNT PAID ANNUALLY	TOTAL ANNUAL AMOUNT
SOURCES:			
Gross wages: husband	_____	_____	_____
Gross wages: wife	_____	_____	_____
Dividends	_____	_____	_____
Dividends	_____	_____	_____
Dividends	_____	_____	_____
Interest	_____	_____	_____
Interest	_____	_____	_____
Rents (cash flow)	_____	_____	_____
Business	_____	_____	_____
Pensions & annuities	_____	_____	_____
Other	_____	_____	_____
Other	_____	_____	_____
Other	_____	_____	_____
Total Gross Income	_____	_____	_____

Once the income is determined, the next step is to determine where it goes. Begin with giving.

Exhibit B: Your Giving

Project your giving for the year by considering each organization you support. This can be from pledges, percentages of income, past giving, or specific giving goals. You may want to check your actual giving to date and then project what you plan to give for the rest of the year.

Your Projected Giving

ORGANIZATION	MONTHLY	ANNUAL	TOTAL
Church	_____	_____	_____
Other	_____	_____	_____
Other	_____	_____	_____
Other	_____	_____	_____
Other	_____	_____	_____
Other	_____	_____	_____
Other	_____	_____	_____
TOTAL	_____	_____	_____

Exhibit C: Taxes

1. The best source for determining taxes is from paystubs. Use the tax withholdings per check and multiply by the number of pay periods per year as described in Exhibit A.
2. Do not be concerned at this time with any tax refunds you may have received. The chief concern is with present cash flow.
3. If you are self-employed or have self-employment income, you will need to estimate your annual taxes. As an alternative you may want to use the total taxes that you paid last year.
4. Self-employment and Social Security taxes can be determined from the following chart:

Social Security Chart

Year	Wage Base	Employee Rate	Maximum Payments	Self Employment Rate	Maximum Payments
1990	$51,300	7.65%	$3,924.45	15.30%	$7,848.90
1991	53,400[1]	7.65%	4,085.10	15.30%	8,170.20
1992	55,536[1,2]	7.65%	4,248.50	15.30%	8,497.00
1993	57,757[1,2]	7.65%	4,418.41	15.30%	8,836.82
1994	60,067[1,2]	7.65%	4,595.12	15.30%	9,190.25
1995	62,470[1,2]	7.65%	4,778.95	15.30%	9,557.91

[1]Effective January 1, 1991, the 1.45% Medicare payroll tax extends from the current year's wage base to $125,000.
[2]Assuming 4% inflation rate.

Your Tax Summary

DEDUCTIONS AND WITHHOLDINGS	MONTHLY	ANNUAL	TOTAL ANNUAL
Federal income tax—husband			
Federal income tax—wife			
State & city income tax—husband			
State & city income tax—wife			
Social security—husband			
Social security—wife			
Total Tax			

Exhibit D: Debt Repayment

1. Don't forget to adjust for any debts that will be completely repaid during the year. For example, if your debt will be paid off in ten months, multiply the monthly amount by 10 rather than by 12.
2. Do not include your mortgage payment. You will include your mortgage payment as a monthly living expense.

Your Debt Repayment

Creditor	Balance Due	Interest Rate	Payment Schedule Per month	Until when
1.	$		$	
2.				
3.				
4.				
5.				
6.				
7.				
8.				
9.				
10.				
Totals	$		$	

Exhibit E: Living Expenses

1. Many expenses, such as utilities, should be monthly averages.
2. Repairs and maintenance can be expressed as a percentage of the monthly mortgage payment. As a general rule, 5% of the monthly mortgage payment x 12 months would be a good estimate for annual home repairs and maintenance.
3. Major purchase of household items such as furnishings, improvements, and the like, should be made from your margin.
4. Note that transportation expense does not include auto payments. Auto payments will be accounted for as a debt.
5. Monthly credit card payments are considered under debts.
6. *Most importantly,* use estimates if you are unsure exactly what is being spent. The objective is to try to be 80 percent accurate on your initial try.

Living Expenses

YEAR: _____	Amount Paid Monthly	Amount Paid Other Than Monthly	Total Annual Amount
HOUSING	_____	_____	_____
Mortgage/rent	_____	_____	_____
Insurance	_____	_____	_____
Property taxes	_____	_____	_____
Electricity	_____	_____	_____
Heating	_____	_____	_____
Water	_____	_____	_____
Sanitation	_____	_____	_____
Telephone	_____	_____	_____
Cleaning	_____	_____	_____
Repairs/maintenance	_____	_____	_____
Improvements	_____	_____	_____
Furnishings	_____	_____	_____
Supplies	_____	_____	_____
Other	_____	_____	_____
Total Housing	_____	_____	_____

FOOD _____ _____ _____

CLOTHING _____ _____ _____
Husband _____ _____ _____
Wife _____ _____ _____
Children _____ _____ _____

Total Clothing _____ _____ _____

TRANSPORTATION _____ _____ _____
Insurance _____ _____ _____
Gas & oil _____ _____ _____
Repairs/maintenance _____ _____ _____
Parking _____ _____ _____
Mass transit or commute _____ _____ _____
Other _____ _____ _____

Total Transportation _____ _____ _____

ENTERTAINMENT/RECREATION _____ _____ _____
Eating out _____ _____ _____
Babysitters _____ _____ _____
Magazines/newspapers/cable _____ _____ _____
Vacation _____ _____ _____
Clubs/activities _____ _____ _____
Classes/courses _____ _____ _____
Other _____ _____ _____

Total Entertainment _____ _____ _____

MEDICAL EXPENSES _____ _____ _____
Insurance _____ _____ _____
Doctors _____ _____ _____
Dentists _____ _____ _____
Drugs _____ _____ _____

Total Medical Expenses _____ _____ _____

INSURANCE _____ _____ _____
Life _____ _____ _____

Disability   _____   _____   _____
Other   _____   _____   _____

Total Insurance   _____   _____   _____

CHILDREN   _____   _____   _____
School lunches   _____   _____   _____
Allowances   _____   _____   _____
Tuition   _____   _____   _____
Lessons   _____   _____   _____
Other   _____   _____   _____

Total Children   _____   _____   _____

GIFTS/SPECIAL OCCASIONS   _____   _____   _____
Christmas   _____   _____   _____
Birthdays   _____   _____   _____
Anniversary   _____   _____   _____
Holidays other than Christmas   _____   _____   _____
Other   _____   _____   _____

Total Gifts   _____   _____   _____

MISCELLANEOUS   _____   _____   _____
Toiletries   _____   _____   _____
Husband: lunches, etc.   _____   _____   _____
Wife: miscellaneous   _____   _____   _____
Dry cleaning/laundry   _____   _____   _____
Animal care   _____   _____   _____
Beauty/barber   _____   _____   _____
Other   _____   _____   _____
Other   _____   _____   _____

Total Miscellaneous   _____   _____   _____

TOTAL LIVING EXPENSES   _____   _____   _____

ANALYZING WHERE IT GOES

Each area of the cash flow process has been determined. The next step will be to transfer the results to the Cash Flow Analysis on pages 79–80 so that each area can be viewed in light of the overall picture.

The number of primary interest is the Cash Flow Margin. Margin represents the resources available for you to use in meeting your long-term goals. You will want to note the section for listing existing margin commitments. These include payroll deductions for retirement programs, annuities, stock purchase plans or any investments which require regular payments. Funds allocated to credit unions, payroll savings plans or deposited to savings accounts are uncommitted funds, since they have no specific purpose and could be reallocated.

Uncommitted margin is the discretionary funds that are available for use in meeting long-term objectives. If you, like Bob and Laura, discover a negative margin after completing your cash flow analysis, don't try to address that this week! Remember, we are not trying to work on solutions at this time. You have something much more important before you begin that part of the process.

Your Cash-Flow Analysis

DATE: _____

GROSS INCOME (Exhibit A page 73) .... $_____

LESS:

    Giving (Exhibit B page 74) $

    Taxes (Exhibit C page 75)

    Debt (Exhibit D page 75)   _____

        Total Expenses .... (_____)

        Net Spendable Income .... $_____
        (Gross Income Less Expenses)

    Living Expenses (Exhibit E pages 76–78)

        Housing   _____

        Food   _____

        Clothing   _____

        Transportation   _____

Entertainment/recreation   _____
Medical   _____
Insurance   _____
Children   _____
Gifts   _____
Miscellaneous   _____

    Total Living Expenses . . . . $(_____)

    Cash Flow Margin . . . . $(_____)
    (Net Spendable Less Living Expenses)

EXISTING MARGIN COMMITMENTS:

_____   _____

_____   _____

_____   _____

    Total Commitments   _____

    UNCOMMITTED MARGIN $_____

A BRIEF SUMMARY

- You have learned the four biblical principles of finance.
- You have determined your net worth.
- You have committed your net worth and all other possessions to God in a specific act of stewardship.
- You have determined your income and have looked at how the income is used in the various areas of the cash-flow process.
- You have determined your annual uncommitted cash margin or your negative cash flow.

You have completed your fact gathering. Now you will turn your attention to determining where you want to go from here.

IN PREPARATION FOR YOUR NEXT SESSION

Spend a few minutes each day reading this verse from Jeremiah. You may want to copy the verse on an index card and keep it with you during the day, or post it in a prominent place in your home (on your refrigerator or your desk, on the mirror in your bathroom, etc.).

For I know the plans I have for you, says the LORD, plans for welfare and not for evil, to give you a future and a hope. Then you will call upon me and come and pray to me, and I will hear you. You will seek me and find me; when you seek me with all your heart.

—Jeremiah 29:11–14, RSV

WEEK FOUR

Where Do I Want to Go?

Setting Faith Financial Goals

"I'm going to go into business for myself, no matter what!" Bob asserted.

"Honey, what are you saying? This is stupid," Laura said.

"What's stupid?"

"We're not in a financial position for you to do that right now," Laura replied.

"And why not?"

"Because we're broke, that's why! Most of what we have has come from borrowing. We've got boat loans, furniture loans, car loans. We're in the hole. When and how are we going to pay those off, especially if you quit your job?" Laura asked.

Laura is asking a valid question. The only way to get from where you are to where you want to go is to develop a plan. Unless you take intentional, deliberate, pro-active steps to address your financial situation, the debt will not disappear, the investments will not happen, and your financial future will happen by default rather than by design.

When my third daughter was nine years old, she learned a valuable, though painfully disappointing, lesson regarding financial choices.

Standing in a store with overpriced notions, such as crazy pens, note-paper, and stickers, her eyes sparkled, wide with excitement. She had found something she absolutely loved. With twenty-five dollars to spend, she could hardly contain her excitement.

We were on a "daddy/daughter date." Our morning at the shopping mall was one of her Christmas gifts. Each year I give my children a sheet of paper as a Christmas gift. On the paper I list several things we can do together during the next year. The list includes outings, such as going out for breakfast or lunch, going to a professional sporting event, or going with me on one of my speaking trips—the choice is theirs.

The first year we began this tradition, Karen chose "spending four hours with me and having twenty-five dollars to spend in any way you choose." She carefully planned our time together: We were to start at the mall on a Saturday morning and end with lunch. The day arrived and she was filled with anticipation.

Picture in your mind a nine-year-old girl with twenty-five dollars in her hand, entering a mall with tens of millions of dollars worth of goods available to buy. The choices awaiting her were seemingly unlimited.

After shopping for just a little while, we found ourselves in the store with the brightly colored, captivating stationery items and she responded to the urge that whispers, "Buy me! Buy me!"

"Karen," I cautioned, "remember that good decision making requires a long-term perspective. Tomorrow these things will not be nearly so attractive." With all the persuasive charms of a nine-year-old, she assured me vehemently that she would use and love these items "forever and forever." When the clerk totaled the bill, she had spent her twenty-five dollars—and we still had three hours left and lunch to buy. We ended up going home early so that she could play with her purchases.

The dilemma she faced is exactly the same dilemma that you and I face—there is *never* enough money to do or buy everything we want. *There are always more ways to spend money than there is money available to spend.* We too often respond no differently than my daughter did: Buy now, regret later.

The very next day, everything Karen had purchased was either used up, broken, or uninteresting. I will never forget her sheepishly admitting to me that she had, in effect, responded to the impulse of the moment and later realized she had made a poor choice. The problem was that her money and time were both irretrievably lost.

What was not lost, however, was the experience and what it taught her. Now, when I am getting ready to buy something, she frequently says to me,

"Daddy, don't forget that the longer term your perspective, the better your decision is likely to be." Sometimes I wish I hadn't taught her that! Nonetheless, Karen learned as a nine-year-old four truths of financial planning that many adults never learn:

- All of us have limited resources.
- There are always more uses of money available than money available to use.
- A dollar spent today is gone—and can never be used in the future for anything else. Today's decisions determine tomorrow's consequences.
- The longer the term of perspective, the better the decision making.

Karen's experience represents the "American way." Most of us are responders, rather than planners. The reason advertisers continue spending billions of dollars annually to entice us to buy things we don't need is because *we continue to buy things we don't need.* We respond to the persuasion and pressure of friends, advertising, and our own emotions rather than plan our spending. Yet a plan without goals is like a runner running a race without a finish line. Have you ever seen a sprinter start down the track and stop and look for the finish line? Of course not! Sprinters know exactly where they are headed, and all of their efforts are directed toward that goal.

We all set goals and objectives and develop plans to achieve them. None of us ever start a vacation without knowing where we want to go; or plan a garden without knowing what we want to come up; or build a home without giving the architect and builder any instructions. Almost anyone would say that goals are important, and yet studies have shown that less than 3 percent of Americans have written goals.

Financial planning is allocating limited financial resources among various alternatives. When we know for certain what financial resources we have and plan to use them to accomplish various goals and objectives, our lives take on the contentment of having made order out of chaos. Our frustration and confusion in having to choose among the overwhelming multiplicity of alternatives disappears. We are freed from short-term pressures; we are free to be different.

As Karen learned, we need to take a long-term perspective in determining our spending decisions—and a long-term perspective must begin with our goals.

During our session this week, we will look at the four reasons setting goals is vital, the reasons why we don't set goals, and then the practical application of setting faith goals.

FOUR VITAL REASONS FOR GOALS

- Goals provide direction and purpose.
- Goals help to crystallize our thinking.
- Goals provide personal motivation.
- Goals become a statement of God's will for our lives.

When I went to Indiana University in 1960 I had an objective: it was to have a good time. I accomplished that objective, but in the process I was asked a couple of times to leave school. My grade-point average hovered around the failing level. When I came back to school, met my future wife, and began to think about marriage, I also began to think about career objectives. I set a goal to become a CPA. My grade-point average went from failing to almost straight A's, and I ultimately graduated from graduate school with honors.

After college, when I was interviewing for jobs, I was often asked by the interviewers what happened. The only thing I could tell them was that I finally had a goal. I had not changed personally, but the goal toward which I was moving had changed and so provided motivation in another direction.

When we set goals, we are involved in purpose as opposed to activities. Our choices for activity become purposeful with more potential for being God-directed. Otherwise, we will continue to be responders—with circumstances, other people, and feelings determining where we wind up.

My wife and I often challenge each other with the statement, "If you aim at nothing, you will hit it every time." Setting goals, *and putting them in writing,* crystallizes your thinking about what you really want to accomplish.

However, the most important reason for setting goals is the spiritual implication. Goals are stated as future objectives, and only God lives in the future. When I set a goal, I have implicitly made a statement that says, "God willing, I believe I should achieve the following . . ." Otherwise, for a Christian, a goal is a presumption.

Few individuals would disagree that goals are important, so why, then, don't we set goals?

BARRIERS TO GOAL SETTING

Many of us don't set goals because we fear failure. If a goal is not set, there is no chance of failing to meet it. Yet a Christian, in the mere act of becoming a Christian, has admitted the inability to govern his or her life. However, the *fear of failure* is so dominant a part of our culture that it, maybe more than any other barrier, is a reason why few people set goals.

The second reason we don't set goals is the *false assumption that goal setting must take a great deal of time*. A little book entitled *Tyranny of the Urgent* by Charles E. Hummel has as its thesis that we get involved in urgent but trivial matters and leave the really important things undone. We often treat goal setting like that. Even if it took a substantial amount of time, it would be worth setting aside the time. As a matter of fact, right now as you read this section, you are aware of certain goals or dreams you've often thought about. We spend much of our lives thinking about goals and dreams, but because we never write them down, we never move toward accomplishing them. The actual process of writing down goals takes only a few minutes. We are merely getting them out of our heads and onto paper.

The third reason that goals are not set is a legitimate one—*we don't know what goals to set*. This is especially true in the financial area because so much advice is being given, both good and bad, that we become confused.

I used to play golf in a very competitive environment with my partners and staff members in the CPA firm. On one occasion we were playing to a hole with an elevated green. We could only "see" the hole from the fairway by seeing the top of the flagstick indicating where the hole was. As our foursome finished the hole, one of us took the flagstick and stuck it in the soft ground on the edge of the green near a sand trap. Well you can imagine what happened. The following foursome, not being able to see the hole, all placed their shots to the flagstick and ended up in the sand trap.

Like that foursome, you may have a good game plan for achieving a goal and take the right steps to achieve it, but if the goal is a wrong one, then the results can be disastrous. It is vitally important to know what goals to set; otherwise, your activity will be channeled in the wrong direction.

Finally, we do not set goals because *many of us do not know how*. We've never learned a goal-setting process. As I said earlier, most of us are lousy money managers, not because we don't want to be good money managers, but because we've never been taught. I have frequently referred to the Financial Planning Diagram (see page 33). Once again, if you examine the diagram, you readily see that there are only eleven goal areas: five short-term and six long-term. This process of financial planning will enable you to clarify your goals and priorities. As Christians we can determine with assurance which goals to set, we can set them, and then we can develop a plan of action to achieve them. Once you know where you are, where you are going, and the steps to take to get there, you will have made a major step toward being a planner rather than a responder.

What's Stopping You?

Review the reasons most of us fail to set goals, then spend some time reflecting on what is stopping you. Then complete this statement:

I haven't put my dreams or goals in writing because _____

_____

_____

_____

_____

Psalm 37:4–5 says, "Delight yourself also in the LORD,/And He shall give you the desires of your heart./Commit your way to the LORD,/Trust also in Him,/ And He shall bring it to pass." What does this verse say to you about "the desires of your heart"? _____

_____

_____

_____

_____

_____

What Not to Do

When we learn the process of how to set goals from a faith perspective, we need to look at four things *not to do*. Isaiah 43:18 says, "Do not remember the former things,/Nor consider the things of old." In setting a goal, first of all, do not focus on the past. Focusing on the past tends to limit our thinking to our past experiences and our past failures. More importantly, focusing on the past leaves God out of the process. "Now to Him who is able to do exceedingly abundantly above all that we ask or think, according to the power that works in us" (Eph. 3:20). God is never limited by what has gone on in the past and wants to do something beyond what we can even think or imagine.

In Luke 1:18 we read the question of Zacharias to the angel in the temple: "How shall I know this? For I am an old man, and my wife is well advanced in years." Zacharias was focusing on his present resources, and that is the second thing we do not want to do in setting a goal. Focusing on our present resources is another way we limit God. The real question is, "What are God's resources?" Recall again Ephesians 3:20: "[God] is able to do exceedingly abundantly above all that we ask or think." What He can do is not limited by my present resources. It is only limited by His resources.

The last thing not to do in setting goals relates to those who are married. A couple should never set a goal apart from or in disagreement with one another. Most women will become widows, and if a woman has not been involved in the goal-setting process, the consequences can be devastating for both the woman and for the family. God puts a man and a woman together to build something new, not to put two competing individuals together so that one can force goals and objectives upon the other. I like what my friend and advisor, Dr. Howard Hendricks, says, "God did not give us a spouse to frustrate us, but to complete us." In the marriage relationship, a couple can set goals that are unique to the couple, not to one of the individuals in the marriage. "Be of the same mind toward one another" (Rom. 12:16). Goal setting is a prayerful process. It is a time for discussion between husbands and wives. I suggest spouses start by first considering their goals separately and then discuss them together to reach a common set of priorities.

And most importantly, *do not skip the goal-setting process just to get on with the financial planning*. Without the goals, your financial plan becomes simply another arithmetic project.

Looking at the Spiritual Fathers

The Bible gives us vivid examples of God's people who lived by setting faith goals. Read Hebrews 11, below. Then, record your thoughts here by completing this statement:

Even though I don't see how it could ever happen, I've always wanted to

_____

_____

_____

_____

_____

[1]Now faith is the substance of things hoped for, the evidence of things not seen. [2]For by it the elders obtained a *good* testimony.

[3]By faith we understand that the worlds were framed by the word of God, so that the things which are seen were not made of things which are visible.

[4]By faith Abel offered to God a more excellent sacrifice than Cain, through which he obtained witness that he was righteous, God testifying of his gifts; and through it he being dead still speaks.

[5]By faith Enoch was taken away so that he did not see death, *"and was not found, because God had taken him";[a]* for before he was taken he had this testimony, that he pleased God. [6]But without faith *it is* impossible to please *Him,* for he who comes to God must believe that He is, and *that* He is a rewarder of those who diligently seek Him.

[7]By faith Noah, being divinely warned of things not yet seen, moved with godly fear, prepared an ark for the saving of his household, by which he condemned the world and became heir of the righteousness which is according to faith.

[8]By faith Abraham obeyed when he was called to go out to the place which he would receive as an inheritance. And he went out, not knowing where he was going. [9]By faith he dwelt in the land of promise as *in* a foreign country, dwelling in tents with Isaac and Jacob, the heirs with him of the same promise; [10]for he waited for the city which has foundations, whose builder and maker *is* God.

[11]By faith Sarah herself also received strength to conceive seed, and she bore a child[a] when she was past the age, because she judged Him faithful who had promised. [12]Therefore from one man, and

him as good as dead, were born *as many* as the stars of the sky in multitude—innumerable as the sand which is by the seashore.

[13]These all died in faith, not having received the promises, but having seen them afar off were assured of them,[a] embraced *them* and confessed that they were strangers and pilgrims on the earth. [14]For those who say such things declare plainly that they seek a homeland. [15]And truly if they had called to mind that *country* from which they had come out, they would have had opportunity to return. [16]But now they desire a better, that is, a heavenly *country.* Therefore God is not ashamed to be called their God, for He has prepared a city for them.

[17]By faith Abraham, when he was tested, offered up Isaac, and he who had received the promises offered up his only begotten *son,* [18]of whom it was said, *"In Isaac your seed shall be called,"*[a] [19]concluding that God *was* able to raise *him* up, even from the dead, from which he also received him in a figurative sense.

[20]By faith Isaac blessed Jacob and Esau concerning things to come.

[21]By faith Jacob, when he was dying, blessed each of the sons of Joseph, and worshiped, *leaning* on the top of his staff.

[22]By faith Joseph, when he was dying, made mention of the departure of the children of Israel, and gave instructions concerning his bones.

[23]By faith Moses, when he was born, was hidden three months by his parents, because they saw *he was* a beautiful child; and they were not afraid of the king's command.

[24]By faith Moses, when he became of age, refused to be called the son of Pharaoh's daughter, [25]choosing rather to suffer affliction with the people of God than to enjoy the passing pleasures of sin, [26]esteeming the reproach of Christ greater riches than the treasures in[a] Egypt; for he looked to the reward.

[27]By faith he forsook Egypt, not fearing the wrath of the king; for he endured as seeing Him who is invisible. [28]By faith he kept the Passover and the sprinkling of blood, lest he who destroyed the firstborn should touch them.

[29]By faith they passed through the Red Sea as by dry *land, whereas* the Egyptians, attempting *to do* so, were drowned.

[30]By faith the walls of Jericho fell down after they were encir-

cled for seven days. [31]By faith the harlot Rahab did not perish with those who did not believe, when she had received the spies with peace.

[32]And what more shall I say? For the time would fail me to tell of Gideon and Barak and Samson and Jephthah, also *of* David and Samuel and the prophets: [33]who through faith subdued kingdoms, worked righteousness, obtained promises, stopped the mouths of lions, [34]quenched the violence of fire, escaped the edge of the sword, out of weakness were made strong, became valiant in battle, turned to flight the armies of the aliens. [35]Women received their dead raised to life again.

Others were tortured, not accepting deliverance, that they might obtain a better resurrection. [36]Still others had trial of mockings and scourgings, yes, and of chains and imprisonment. [37]They were stoned, they were sawn in two, were tempted,[a] were slain with the sword. They wandered about in sheepskins and goatskins, being destitute, afflicted, tormented— [38]of whom the world was not worthy. They wandered in deserts and mountains, *in* dens and caves of the earth.

[39]And all these, having obtained a good testimony through faith, did not receive the promise. [40]God having provided something better for us, that they should not be made perfect apart from us.

WHAT IS A FAITH GOAL?

A faith goal will typically have three characteristics. The first characteristic is that *its means of accomplishment may not be evident*. You may not be able to see how it will happen. "By faith Noah, being divinely warned of things not yet seen, moved with godly fear, prepared an ark for the saving of his household" (Heb. 11:7). Noah had never seen rain and certainly did not know how God was going to send a universal flood, but in response to God's initiative, Noah prepared an ark. He had faith that God was going to do what He said He was going to do.

Second, a faith goal may, in many cases, *be set with inadequate resources*. A story similar to that of Zacharias in the temple is found in Hebrews 11:11. "By faith Sarah herself also received strength to conceive seed, and she bore a child when she was past the age, because she judged Him faithful who had promised." Setting a faith goal may mean there are "apparently" no adequate resources to accomplish that goal. If it is God's goal, it is God's responsibility to provide the resources.

Of course, you do not test God by dreaming up goals; that is why the *process* of setting the goal is so important. When you spend time with Him, you receive assurance and conviction that this is what He would have you do. Therefore, resources are of no concern. They are God's responsibility. You do not set the goal and then go to Him asking for the resources. You let Him speak to you and develop the goal, and then you trust Him for the resources.

A faith goal will typically require setting an objective *without fully understanding it*. "By faith Abraham obeyed when he was called to go out to the place which he would afterward receive as an inheritance. And he went out, not knowing where he was going" (Heb. 11:8). Abraham did not know where he was going, but he went in response to God's initiative. The goals that you set by faith in the financial area of your life may also need to be set without full understanding about how they will be achieved with present resources. But many of the heroes of faith in Hebrews 11 experienced the same uncertainty.

Setting a faith goal is answering the question, "God, what are your plans?" or saying, "God, I'm available—not necessarily able—but available." I define a faith goal as an objective toward which I believe God wants me to move. A simple four-step process will enable you to determine your faith goals.

SETTING YOUR FAITH GOALS

1. Spend Time with God

One of our critical needs in the Christian life is to spend time with our Lord in communion with Him, seeking His will and direction. You have been reading the verse from Jeremiah during this past week. God's Word clearly says that if we seek His direction and will, He will respond by giving us that direction.

Spending time with God is essential; otherwise, goal setting without God's direction becomes merely striving after our own dreams and desires. A faith goal is a statement of God's will.

2. Record the Impressions

As you spend time with God, you need to record what He seems to be saying to you. You need to take the second step, because over time, as you record the impressions you receive, assurance and conviction will result. "Now faith is the substance of things hoped for, the evidence of things not seen" (Heb. 11:1). You need to be continually asking God, "What would You have me do?" But not, "How would You have me to do it?" As you record the answers He gives you, you become more and more sure of the goal. It is essential to have the goal recorded, because very likely there will be testing. God's objective is to build your faith, and testing does it!

3. Make the Goal Measurable

After spending time with God and recording what He seems to be saying to you, you are ready to set a faith goal. The objective toward which you believe God wants you to move must be *measurable*. For example, to be a good father is not a goal, but a purpose statement. To spend fifteen minutes a day with each of my children is a goal. That can be measured. Because goals are measurable, we know definitely when they have been achieved. If you cannot determine when a goal has been achieved, then it was not a goal—it was an intention or a purpose statement.

I really must stress the importance of making goals measurable. A measurable goal gives a standard of accountability. If the goal is not measurable, you have no way to assess when you've achieved it and the goal then becomes meaningless.

Once you have spent time with God, recorded what He seems to be saying to you, and set a measurable objective, you have a faith goal: an objective toward which we believe God wants us to move.

4. Take Action

Faith, in itself, is *acting* on the basis of what God wants you to do. *Faith* is an action word.

What is required on your part is two things: First, trust that God will do His part, and second, take action. Taking action does not mean we have to do it all. Biblically, we are called to *simply take the first step*. Abraham, Noah, Sarah, Nehemiah, Daniel, and David all exercised faith by taking a first step of action in complete dependence upon God—without full understanding, adequate resources, or seeing how their goal could be accomplished. What was required of them was merely the first step. God then showed the second step, and then the third, and then the fourth. God leads us one step at a time.

Again, the order of the *process* is essential:

- Spend time with God.
- Record what He is saying to you.
- Set a measurable goal.
- Take the first step.

God may not accomplish the goal in the way that you think He should do it, or in the way that you would do it. Give God the flexibility to do things His way, with His timing and His resources.

When I was initially developing the concepts and philosophy of biblical financial planning, I shared with my family this goal setting process. At that time, our church was having a missions conference, and our daughter Denise wanted to make a pledge to the missions committee. She assured my wife and me that she had gone through the process of spending time with God, recording what He had said, and felt that He would have her pledge two dollars a week. As my wife and I discussed it, we realized we had a problem since our daughter only received an allowance of one dollar a week. My wife and I spent an afternoon trying to determine how we were going to "help God out" and keep Him from being embarrassed, because, obviously, Denise could not fulfill that pledge. After a while, we realized what we were doing and stepped back to see what God would do.

Six months passed and I had forgotten about the pledge. One day my wife asked me if I realized that Denise had made her pledge of two dollars every week. By the end of the year, she had literally given $104. I know that money did not come out of her savings account, because I controlled that account. Frankly, I don't know where the money came from—and it is not important. The point is that she did what she believed God would have her do—one step at a time. She did not have to see how it was going to be accomplished, and she did not have to have the resources, nor did she have to understand the process of financial planning in order to get it accomplished. At the end of the year, the pledge was fulfilled, her spiritual growth was hastened, and God received the glory.

As adults, we too often think a goal is insurmountable, and in so doing we forget who it came from. God is not limited by inadequate resources or seemingly insurmountable obstacles. God is limited only by our willingness to be faithful—our willingness to take the first step.

Living by faith is a process and God is always dealing with us during this process. When setting a goal, never set the goal "in concrete." Rather, "write it in sand on the seashore," because He can give us directions more easily when we're flexible than when we're inflexible, refusing to allow Him to change the writing.

To determine specifically where we are going financially, look again at the Financial Planning Diagram on page 33. As we've already determined, there are only six goals that can be set for the long term:

1. Giving;
2. Providing a college education for your children;
3. Paying off debt;
4. Accomplishing lifestyle desires;
5. Beginning your own business;
6. Achieving financial independence.

Each of these goals, because of its financial nature, can be expressed in specific terms, and can therefore meet the criterion of being measurable.

With these six goals in mind, I designed a Vision for the Future Chart with space to answer questions under each goal setting area. Each statement is preceded by: "In five years we see the following taking place." Look at the chart on pages 96 and 97 with Bob and Laura's answers.

Then use the blank chart on pages 98–101 to aid in your goal-setting process. Remember that goal setting is a prayerful process, and is a time for discussion between husband and wife to ensure congruity of goals. For couples, I suggest each of you, independently, consider your personal goals and then discuss them together to come to an agreement on the priorities of the goals. For this purpose, two blank Vision for the Future worksheets are included.

If you do not have specific goals in mind, put down what first comes to your mind as you consider each of the areas shown on the chart. As you pray about these goals, God may lead you to change some or eliminate some. Be flexible and remember that this is the beginning of a process that will continue as long as you live. It cannot be "completed" at a certain point in time. God will reveal to you His priorities regarding your financial goals, and these priorities will be different for each individual and couple. Our financial goals are as unique as we are.

Your first-priority financial goal may be to establish a college fund for your children, but there may not be enough time to save an adequate amount. Your part (the action step) is to open a savings account and to adjust the budget to free up your resources for this purpose as best you can. God's part (and your area of trust) is to provide the resources.

Bob & Laura's Vision for the Future

In five years, we see the following taking place:

GIVING:

_____ We will be giving _____10_____ % per year.
_____ We will be making additional gifts each year of: _____-0-_____ .
_____ We will have made total gifts of: $2,000 for the new chapel.

COLLEGE:

_____ A college fund will exist for each of our children:

Child	Type of College	Approximate Annual Cost	Approximate Total Cost
Sue	State College	$6,000	$24,000

LIFESTYLE DESIRES:

_____ We will have made the following major purchases: (new home, car, vacations, etc.)

Item	Amount
Replace Laura's car	$ 5,000
Redecorate living room	5,000
Buy a new house	20,000

_____ We will have the following type of lifestyle: (increase, decrease, or maintain present level)

Maintain our present lifestyle.

PAY OFF DEBT:

_____ We will have paid off the following debts:

Owed To	Total
Credit cards	$ 3,000
Boat loan	5,000
Bank loan	13,500
Parents' loan	5,000
Auto loan	4,000
Life insurance	5,000

BEGIN BUSINESS:

_____ We will have started our own business which will require an investment of:

_____

_____

FINANCIAL INDEPENDENCE:

_____ We will have the following investments:

Type of Investment	Amount Invested	Annual Return
Emergency fund	$5,000	

_____ I would like to pass on to my spouse (children) the following estate:
$100,000

_____

_____ Support my lifestyle of $_____ per month.

My Vision for the Future

By _____ (date), I see the following taking place:

GIVING:

_____ We will be giving _____% per year.
_____ We will be making additional gifts each year of: _____.
_____ We will have made total gifts of: _____.

COLLEGE:

_____ A college fund will exist for each of our children:

Child	Type of College	Approximate Annual Cost	Approximate Total Cost
_____	_____	_____	_____
_____	_____	_____	_____
_____	_____	_____	_____
_____	_____	_____	_____

LIFESTYLE DESIRES:

_____ We will have made the following major purchases: (new home, car, vacations, etc.)

Item	Amount
_____	_____
_____	_____
_____	_____
_____	_____
_____	_____

_____ We will have the following type of lifestyle: (increase, decrease, or maintain present level)

_____

PAY OFF DEBT:

_____ We will have paid off the following debts:

Owed To	*Total*
_____	_____
_____	_____
_____	_____
_____	_____
_____	_____
_____	_____
_____	_____
_____	_____

BEGIN BUSINESS:

_____ We will have started our own business which will require an investment of:

_____

_____

FINANCIAL INDEPENDENCE:

_____ We will have the following investments:

Type of Investment	*Amount Invested*	*Annual Return*
_____	_____	_____
_____	_____	_____
_____	_____	_____
_____	_____	_____
_____	_____	_____

_____ I would like to pass on to my spouse (children) the following estate:

_____

_____

_____

_____ Support my lifestyle of $_____ per month.

My Vision for the Future

By _____ (date), I see the following taking place:

GIVING:

_____ We will be giving _____ % per year.

_____ We will be making additional gifts each year of: _____.

_____ We will have made total gifts of: _____.

COLLEGE:

_____ A college fund will exist for each of our children:

Child	Type of College	Approximate Annual Cost	Approximate Total Cost
_____	_____	_____	_____
_____	_____	_____	_____
_____	_____	_____	_____
_____	_____	_____	_____

LIFESTYLE DESIRES:

_____ We will have made the following major purchases: (new home, car, vacations, etc.)

Item	Amount
_____	_____
_____	_____
_____	_____
_____	_____
_____	_____

_____ We will have the following type of lifestyle: (increase, decrease, or maintain present level)

_____

PAY OFF DEBT:

_____ We will have paid off the following debts:

Owed To	Total
_____	_____
_____	_____

_____   _____
_____   _____
_____   _____
_____   _____
_____   _____
_____   _____
_____   _____

BEGIN BUSINESS:

_____ We will have started our own business which will require an investment of:

_____
_____

FINANCIAL INDEPENDENCE:

_____ We will have the following investments:

Type of Investment	Amount Invested	Annual Return
_____	_____	_____
_____	_____	_____
_____	_____	_____
_____	_____	_____
_____	_____	_____

_____ I would like to pass on to my spouse (children) the following estate:

_____
_____
_____

_____ Support my lifestyle of $_____ per month.

At this point you know where you are, and you know what God would have you do financially. The next step is to continue the goal-setting process while you begin the action steps to accomplish the goals that God has given you. Remember, you don't have to see _how_. You may not have the resources, yet you can take action without full understanding, trusting that God is in control.

IN PREPARATION FOR YOUR NEXT SESSION

As I said at the beginning of this session, goal setting is a process, one which involves spending time with God, seeking His will and direction, and recording your impressions. Over time you will probably feel your goals changing, evolving. This is a dynamic process, one which is ongoing, not a "once and for all." You may already be spending time daily in prayer, study, and reflection. If not, however, I suggest you begin now the process of seeking God's direction daily. What follows are seven Scripture verses you may want to use during the next week for your quiet time. You may choose to read one a day, and record your thoughts, prayers, and concerns, or you might prefer to use one a week for the duration of this planning process. Read the verse prayerfully, asking God to give you a willing heart and clear direction.

DAY ONE OR WEEK FIVE

Do not remember the former things,
Nor consider the things of old.
Behold, I will do a new thing,
Now it shall spring forth.

—Isaiah 43:18–19

_____

_____

_____

_____

_____

_____

_____

_____

_____

_____

Dear God, we are trying to do everything with our financial decisions, and right now it's hard not to feel at times that we are up against a challenge that's bigger than we are. But we know our financial situation is not bigger than You. We ask that You show us what we are to do first. With Your leading, we are willing. Amen.

DAY TWO OR WEEK SIX

Now to Him who is able to do exceedingly abundantly above all that we ask or think, according to the power that works in us.

—Ephesians 3:20

_____

_____

_____

_____

_____

_____

_____

_____

_____

_____

_____

_____

Dear Lord, You have been faithful to us at every turn. Even in the times we couldn't see Your hand at work, we know You were still present with us. Your love is gentle; Your power is great. Empower us now to be open to Your Spirit. We know our tendency is to put You in a box, a box defined by the limitations of our present situation. God, we ask that You break the constraints of our boxed-in thinking, and open our hearts to Your limitless power. Amen.

DAY THREE OR WEEK SEVEN

Then [Jesus] said to Thomas, "Reach your finger here, and look at My hands. . . . Do not be unbelieving, but believing." And Thomas answered and said to Him, "My Lord and my God!" Jesus said to him, "Thomas, because you have seen Me, you have believed. Blessed are those who have not seen and yet have believed."

—John 20:27–29

Now faith is the substance of things hoped for, the evidence of things not seen.

—Hebrews 11:1

_____

_____

_____

_____

_____

_____

_____

_____

_____

_____

_____

God, we—like Thomas—so long to see and touch You. We long to see Your hand at work. But faith is letting go of *our* need for proof and holding fast to Your promises. Faith is letting You be the Master Designer of our hopes and dreams. Lord, we give You our fears, our anxieties, our willing hearts, knowing that You are leading us, guiding us, preparing us. God, today we ask that You open our eyes to "see" You in the words of a friend, the wonder of a loved face, and in the hidden places of our lives. Amen.

DAY FOUR OR WEEK EIGHT

And my God shall supply all your need according to His riches in glory by Christ Jesus. Now to our God and Father be glory forever and ever.
—Phillippians 4:19–20

_____

_____

_____

_____

_____

_____

_____

_____

_____

_____

_____

_____

_____

_____

_____

_____

_____

God, we allow our "wants" to be confused with "needs." By habit we too casually say we "need" to get thus and so. What we really mean is that we *want* to get that item. Lord, clarify our needs and wants. Enable us to be honest with ourselves, honest with You, and honest with our families. Amen.

DAY FIVE OR WEEK NINE

Trust in the LORD with all your heart,
And lean not on your own understanding;
In all your ways acknowledge Him,
And He shall direct your paths.

—Proverbs 3:5–6

_____

_____

_____

_____

_____

_____

_____

_____

_____

_____

_____

_____

_____

_____

_____

_____

Lord, our understanding is often so clouded, so murky. Pressures, commitments, obligations crowd and clutter our lives. Your calling—Your still, small voice—too easily gets lost in the clamor of our days. Lord, bring stillness to our hearts and clarity to our minds, that we might be faithful as You direct our paths. Amen.

DAY SIX OR WEEK TEN

Keep your life free from love of money, and be content with what you have; for he has said, "I will never fail you nor forsake you."
                                        —Hebrews 13:5 RSV

_____

_____

_____

_____

_____

_____

_____

_____

_____

_____

_____

_____

_____

_____

_____

_____

_____

_____

_____

_____

_____

O Lord, this verse hits so close to home! Only by Your grace can we keep our lives free from the love of money . . . and all the distractions, diversions, and amusements that money will buy. Keep our eyes on You and show us the balance of living joyfully, yet responsibly, as Your sons and daughters in Christ. Amen.

DAY SEVEN OR WEEK ELEVEN

You shall weep no more.
He will be very gracious to you at the sound of your cry;
When He hears it, He will answer you.
                                                    —Isaiah 30:19

_____

_____

_____

_____

_____

_____

_____

_____

_____

_____

_____

_____

_____

_____

_____

Dear God, we've learned through this planning process that money is merely a resource, a means to an end. Yet we so often let money—either the abundance of, the acquisition of, or the lack of it—govern our lives. We have wept tears of frustration at times. Lord, hear our cry as we seek Your will. And by Your gracious, loving Spirit, surround us this day with Your presence that we might walk in Your ways and hear Your call. Amen.

Knowing What to Avoid

The Most Common Financial Mistakes

---

*"We should live and learn. But by the time we've learned,
it's usually too late to live."*

*"It's tough to plan for the future when you're too busy
fixing the things you did yesterday."*

Over the last several years I have had the privilege of traveling all over this country and speaking to literally thousands of people. I have been asked many times what is the biggest financial mistake I see, and the answer is easy—a consumptive lifestyle. A consumptive lifestyle is simply spending more than you can afford. Almost everyone in America falls victim to the temptation of living a consumptive lifestyle.

Not long ago I stopped in a jewelry store to have a ring sized. I was standing at the counter when I noticed a well-dressed young man purchasing a Rolex watch. A Rolex has become—along with a Mercedes or BMW car—a symbol of success. This man was purchasing a relatively inexpensive, $2,000 Rolex (many sell for over $10,000). Yet, I noticed the sales contract was written up for approximately $4,000. I thought there must have been some mistake. But it turned out that the price of the watch was $2,000, and the finance charge was an additional $2,000. This man had purchased the watch with $285 down and a balance payable of $235 per month. When he walked out of the store with that watch on, he was giving the impression that he could afford a Rolex. Yet, could he really?

At this point you may be thinking, "Oh, come on. Everyone borrows and uses credit. If they didn't, no one would be able to afford anything." If you can afford the monthly payments, why not use the convenience of credit cards or consumer financing? Why not enjoy it while you pay for it?

We are a society bombarded with a hedonistic philosophy "Enjoy it now." "You only go around once." "Live it up." "You owe it to yourself."

To understand "why not?" you have to understand what I call the opportunity cost of consumption. A dollar spent today does not take a dollar out of the future; it takes multiple dollars. Only $2.74 per day spent on nonproductive purchases results in an overspending of $1,000 per year. If that $1,000 per year were invested instead, earning 12.5 percent compounded annually (such as in an IRA), then the $2.74 per day actually cost me the $1,000,000 that I *could* have had over a forty-year period.

Does this sound like an exaggeration? Not at all. To realize the opportunity cost of a consumptive lifestyle, we must first understand what has been called the eighth wonder of the world—the "magic of compounding." The magic of compounding can work for you—or against you. But first, before talking about the most common financial mistakes people make or going any further with developing your financial plan, let's look at the phenomenon called compounding.

THE MAGIC OF COMPOUNDING

The magic of compounding results because interest earns interest, which earns interest, which earns interest, which earns interest, ad infinitum. In other words, if you started supporting yourself at age twenty and for the next forty years you spent $1,000 less than you earned and invested that $1,000 each year in an investment, earning at least 12.5% interest, at age sixty you would have an investment fund of $1,000,000. (This computation ignores the tax implications, which we will deal with later.)

The 12.5% and $1,000,000 are not magical nor necessarily even desirable, but they do illustrate the growth potential created by compounding.

Compounding, the relationship between an interest rate and a time period can be determined by the "Rule of 72." The Rule of 72 says that any interest rate divided into 72 will always give you the length of time required for an amount to double in value. For example, if you invest $10,000 at an interest rate of 3%, it will take twenty-four years for the $10,000 to grow to $20,000.

$$3\% \overline{)\,72} \quad \frac{24 \text{ years}}{}$$

If, however, I can earn 6%, the $10,000 will double in only twelve years.

$$6\% \overline{)\,72} \quad \frac{12 \text{ years}}{}$$

To observe the magic of compounding, observe in the table on page 113 that as you double the interest rate earned, you get a geometric increase in the amount accumulated.

How important is the interest rate? Look again at the table on page 113. At 25 percent, $10,000 grows to $75,231,638 in forty years, but at 24 percent, it only grows to $54,559,126 in the same length of time, nearly $21,000,000 difference resulting from only 1 percent difference in the interest rate. In other words, the amount is not nearly so important as the interest rate and the time period. The earlier you start and the more you earn in interest, the less you need to start with.

When you look at financial tables on page 113 and compare the deposit of an annual amount with the deposit of a lump sum, you immediately see that it takes much more money over a longer time period to achieve the same results. Ten thousand dollars invested initially and never added to, but growing at a compounded rate of 25 percent per year, grows to $75,231,638; whereas $1,000 invested per year for 40 years or a total of $40,000 invested (four times as much) only "grows" to $30,088,655.

Here is the key point: *You do not have to save $1,000,000 to end up with $1,000,000.* The earlier you start, the less you have to save. The later you start, the more you either have to save or earn in interest (and therefore take more risk).

Principles of Financial Success

The retired pastor I mentioned in Part One, who had never earned more than $8,000 in any given year, achieved an incredible level of financial suc-

How to Become a Millionaire

DEPOSIT A LUMP SUM OF $10,000:
END OF YEAR VALUES

	5	10	15	20	25	30	35	40
2%	$11,040	$12,189	$13,458	$14,859	$16,406	$18,113	$19,998	$22,080
4%	12,166	14,802	18,009	21,911	26,658	32,433	39,460	48,010
6%	13,382	17,908	23,969	32,071	42,918	57,434	76,860	102,857
8%	14,693	21,589	31,721	46,609	68,484	100,626	147,853	217,245
10%	16,105	25,937	41,772	67,274	108,347	174,494	281,024	492,592
12%	17,623	31,058	54,735	96,462	170,000	299,599	527,996	930,509
14%	19,254	37,072	71,379	137,434	264,619	509,501	981,001	1,888,835
16%	21,003	44,114	92,655	193,607	408,742	858,498	1,803,140	3,787,211
18%	22,877	52,338	119,737	273,930	626,686	1,433,706	3,279,972	7,503,783
20%	24,883	61,917	154,070	383,375	953,962	2,373,763	5,906,682	14,697,606
22%	27,027	73,046	197,422	533,576	1,442,101	3,897,578	10,534,018	28,470,377
24%	29,317	85,944	251,956	738,641	2,165,419	6,348,199	18,610,540	54,559,126
26%	30,517	93,132	284,217	867,361	2,646,698	8,077,935	24,651,903	75,231,638

$1,000 DEPOSITED EACH YEAR:
END OF YEAR VALUES

	5	10	15	20	25	30	35	40
5%	$5,225	$12,578	$21,578	$33,065	$47,727	$66,439	$90,320	$120,800
8%	5,867	14,487	27,152	45,762	73,106	113,283	172,317	259,056
12%	6,353	17,548	37,279	72,052	133,333	241,332	431,663	767,091
16%	6,877	21,321	51,660	115,380	249,214	530,312	1,120,713	2,360,757
20%	7,442	25,959	72,035	186,688	471,981	1,181,882	2,948,341	7,343,858
24%	8,048	31,643	100,815	303,600	898,092	2,640,916	7,750,225	22,728,802

cess by practicing five key principles of financial success and allowing the magic of compounding to work for him.

1. He understood biblical principles.
2. He lived a nonconsumptive lifestyle.
3. He avoided the use of debt.
4. He maintained high liquidity.
5. He set long-term goals.

However, to go back to my initial question, "If you can afford the monthly payments, why not enjoy it while you pay for it?" let's turn compounding around and see what happens when it works against you.

If you purchase a car for $10,000, with financing at 12.5 percent over four years, you will be paying a monthly payment of $265.80. At the end of four years, you will have paid $12,758.40 for the car. That doesn't seem so bad, does it?

Now if you purchase another car in four years through financing and continue to do this over a working life of forty years, you will have purchased ten cars and paid car payments totaling $127,584 ($12,758.40 x 10 = $127.584). The bank received $265.80 per month for 480 months and never had at risk any more than $10,000; they in turn reinvested that $265.80 in other loans yielding 12.5 percent, so that they accumulated $3,641,550 on your total payments of $127,584. What if, instead of making car payments, you paid yourself $265.80 per month and were able to invest that payment at 12.5 percent? Then *you* would have the $3,641,550, not the lending institution! The true cost of driving those cars is $2,641,550, not $127,584!

Don't get me wrong. I am *not* against buying a new car, and later in this chapter, I'll outline the most economical way to do so. The point I'm making is that *consumption has a staggering cost*—a much higher cost than many have ever realized.

The magic of compounding will work for you instead of against you, *only* if you spend less than you earn. To say it another way, in order to achieve your long-term goals, you must have a positive cash-flow margin.

At this point, you may be asking yourself:

- Why didn't I hear this earlier? It's too late for me.
- Yes, but where can I earn 25 percent?
- With inflation, how much will $75,000,000 be worth in forty years?
- But what about taxes on the interest every year? After paying the taxes, compounding won't yield that much.
- So who cares about the future? I want to enjoy my money now.

Let me assure you that not only do I understand these questions, but in some cases, I am still dealing with them on a personal level. All of these questions will be addressed as you complete this planning process. However, these issues will not "make or break" you financially. What will have a much greater impact on the financial well-being of most individuals are actually four very simple mistakes. At the completion of this week's session, you will be prioritizing the goals you put in writing last week. Before determining your priorities, let's look at the most common mistakes—mistakes which can easily be avoided by financial planning.

AVOIDING THE MOST COMMON MISTAKES

Mistake #1: Living a Consumptive Lifestyle

Because many of my clients give substantial sums of money away, I was asked by one Christian leader what a million-dollar giver looks like. My response was, "If he looks like he can give a million dollars, he probably can't." The point is that someone whose lifestyle requires substantial expenditures must earn a considerable amount of money to have enough left after taxes to fund that lifestyle. Someone in a 50 percent tax bracket spending $100,000 to live must earn at least $200,000 to have $100,000 left after taxes to spend on that lifestyle. There is no way around that through tax planning, since tax planning requires that money be spent in order to reduce taxes.

I'm well aware that avoiding the use of debt is incredibly difficult. The promotion of credit card use has made credit so easy to obtain and the temptation to use credit or debt overwhelmingly difficult to resist. Credit card companies are spending hundreds of billions of dollars to entice us to use credit cards to make spending "easier," and those amounts are a pittance when compared to the additional advertising dollars of retailers.

When Sears introduced the Discover card, they used Atlanta as a test market. Newspaper articles at the time of its introduction reported that Sears' officials expected credit card usage to go up by *thirty-five billion dollars* as a result of the introduction of the new card. Their studies showed that the card use would be incremental borrowing rather than replacement borrowing. In other words, people would be adding to their already existing credit card debt because the new card was nothing more than an additional line of credit for them.

When you live a consumptive lifestyle, spending more than you can afford by relying on credit cards and consumer lending, *you allow the magic of compounding to work against you*.

I was talking with a banker friend of mine one day about credit card debt and how the banking industry viewed people who paid their debt off every month. He told me that in the banking industry, a person who uses his or her credit card for convenience and pays the debt off each month is known as a "deadbeat." What a difference a few years makes! When I was growing up, a deadbeat was someone who didn't pay his bills; now a deadbeat is someone who does pay his bills and does it promptly! Lending institutions do not want people to pay their credit card debts each month because of the 18–21 percent interest that is earned on that debt.

In working with hundreds of individuals, I've observed that the more television a person watches, the higher lifestyle that person is likely to desire. Television advertising is extremely sophisticated and effective. In a similar way, the more time you spend in shopping malls, the higher lifestyle you'll desire—much like going to the grocery store just before mealtime. Chances are you will spend substantially more than if you went after a meal and with a specific list in hand.

Living expenses and debt go hand in hand. Typically, debt is used to fund living expenses and, conversely, without the ability to borrow, the ability to increase the lifestyle is not there. However, let me say very clearly: *You cannot borrow your way to prosperity*.

Mistake #2: Living Without a Budget

The second most common mistake in the area of living expenses is the lack of a budget. If you have no budget, which is in effect a short-term plan, you are in reality planning to live as a responder. We've all seen parodies of the person who "saves" thousands of dollars buying things on sale that are not needed. But impulsive or responsive spending is not a gender-specific problem. Women tend to buy responsively while shopping—clothes, cosmetics, shoes. But men are equally "guilty" of being "responders." The problem is, we men tend to go for the big ticket items—boats, cars, sporting equipment, investments, and second homes.

The whole idea of living on a budget is distasteful to almost all of us because we view it as constraining. Yet, a budget can be one of the most financially freeing things you can have. A budget guides you and tells you when you are on course, just as a road map does when driving in an unfamiliar area. Not having the map creates fear, perhaps frustration, and certainly anxiety. The same can be said about living without a budget.

A budget is the only way you will be able to generate a positive cash flow—and a positive cash flow margin is *absolutely essential* if you are to accomplish either long-term or short-term financial goals.

The Benefits of a Positive Cash Flow.

Without a cash-flow margin, you cannot accumulate in order to meet long-term goals or accomplish any of the four other short-term goals—tax reduction, increased giving, debt reduction, and increased living expense.

To reduce taxes, either additional expenditures must be made for such things as increased giving, IRA'S, tax-sheltered investments, and the like, or income must be reduced. Either increased deductible expenses or reduced income will result in tax reduction. However, both require that there be a positive cash flow to begin the process.

Without a positive cash flow, increased giving is not an option. Once there is a positive cash flow, however, and it is used to increase giving, that decision results in decreased taxes because charitable contributions are deductible. As a financial planner, I have seen many people plan all of their tax reduction through giving. However, they had to have a cash flow margin to begin the process.

Obviously, if you want to reduce your debt principal payments, you must have the excess cash to do so. If you are "going in the hole" by overspending, then there is no way to get out of debt until you generate a positive cash flow. After debt retirement that extra amount can be used to reduce debt further, which in turn increases the cash flow.

Finally, if a couple or individual has as a short-term goal to increase the level of their lifestyle through a new home purchase, a new car purchase, vacations, additional giving at Christmas, or eating out more often, they must have a positive cash flow to have the additional funds.

When you look at the True Cost of Lifestyle chart on page 118 you see that a couple earning $30,000 a year, tithing 10 percent, paying taxes at the rate of 18 percent, having no debt repayment, and spending $21,600 to live has no cash flow margin. In order to increase their living expenses by $4,800, they must increase their income by $6,800 in order to have, after tithing 10 percent and paying taxes of $1,224, an incremental cash flow of $4,896 with which to fund the increased living expenses.

The True Cost of Living Lifestyle

	Before	After	Increase
Income	$30,000	$36,800	$ 6,800
Tithe @ 10%	(3,000)	(3,680)	(680)
Taxes @ 18%	(5,400)	(6,624)	(1,224)
Debt Repayment	-0-	-0-	-0-
Net Spendable Income	21,600	26,496	4,896
Living Expenses	(21,600)	(26,400)	(4,800)
Cash Flow Margin	$ -0-	$ 96	$ 96

To look at this illustration another way, if this couple were earning $36,800, tithing 10 percent, and paying their taxes, and if they decreased their lifestyle by $4,800, all of that amount would go to the bottom line—the cash flow margin. Therefore, reducing living expenses causes a dollar-for-dollar increase in cash-flow margin, whereas increasing living expenses requires an income increase if there is no beginning cash-flow margin equal to the increase in living expenses plus the taxes and tithe paid on that amount.

This fact is often overlooked when couples plan their expenses. They forget that to fund an increase in one area through the means of increasing income, they must also fund the taxes and tithe paid on that income. Couples deciding that a wife should work in order to have additional money available to spend often overlook this and find themselves going deeper into debt, first of all, by increasing their living expenses by the amount of the increased income, not to mention the additional taxes and tithe.

Let me repeat: debt reduction and lifestyle reduction both have an immediate dollar-for-dollar impact on the cash-flow margin, thereby giving the flexibility to accomplish many other goals such as tax reduction, increased giving, and accumulation.

Mistake #3: Buying and Selling Cars

The third most common mistake in the lifestyle area occurs in buying and selling automobiles. There may be more pride and ego involved in decisions about automobiles than any other financial decisions. A recent quote in a newspaper bears this out: "Logic and automobile purchases do not go hand in hand."

Most of the time when I have the opportunity to speak to groups, I promise to tell them before I am finished the name of the cheapest car they can own. This statement always creates a lot of interest. I learned this information several years ago before I became a Christian. Although I had achieved almost every financial goal I desired, I still wanted to purchase and drive a brand new Cadillac. (This was before the Mercedes and the BMW were status symbols.)

However, I was only thirty years old at the time and felt that driving a new Cadillac would be pretentious and might even be harmful for my business so I purchased an Oldsmobile 98 with all the accessories. At the time, I thought that within a couple of years, "when I was older," I would trade the car in on a new Cadillac. During that time period, however, I became a Christian and my goals and desires changed rather rapidly regarding material possessions. I lost interest in driving a new Cadillac.

As time went on, the Oldsmobile eventually had close to 150,000 miles on it—and looked it. The car had to be replaced. Once you start looking at new automobiles, your tastes change and your desires increase. I found myself looking at new cars in parking lots, on the road while I was driving, stopping at auto dealerships, and in every way lusting after a new car.

I decided at that point to do a study to determine the best car to buy from a strictly economical standpoint, taking into account all of the factors, such as gas mileage, cost of repairs, license cost, financing cost, opportunity cost of the cash paid out, insurance cost and depreciation. I spent hours and hours comparing all the numbers and coming up with a definite conclusion. I found without exception that the cheapest car I could own was that Oldsmobile! Even though the cost of repairs was substantial and gas mileage was incredibly low, they did not offset the much higher costs related to a new car in terms of licenses, insurance, maintenance, depreciation, financing costs, or opportunity costs. Not only was I disappointed that as a CPA I could not economically justify a different car, but I was stunned at the result. I had always assumed that the low-priced, high mileage, foreign cars would be the most economical to own.

After studying this whole issue of buying automobiles, I came to two conclusions: the cheapest car anyone can ever own is always the car they presently own, unless it is sold and the proceeds reinvested in a lower priced car; and the longer a car is driven, the cheaper it becomes to operate.

I did not share these results with very many people until after February 11, 1980, when the *Wall Street Journal* published an article with an analysis of automobile ownership. The article stated that "the longer a car is kept (new or used), the cheaper it becomes to run per mile. . . . Average depreciation of a new car during the first year is 31.5 percent of its purchase price." The article also stated that the typical purchase price for a one- to four-year-old used car ranges from 20 percent to 80 percent below that of a new car. Ten years later the conclusions and numbers have not changed.

One of the ways, then, that living expenses can be decreased most dramatically is by merely deciding to continue driving the car you presently own. If you can also repair it and maintain it yourself, you will over time have substantial cash-flow savings that can be invested for the future rather than consumed in the present.

Another *Wall Street Journal* article entitled, "Riddle: Why Won't a Typical Millionaire Take You for a Ride in His Fancy Car?" appeared in May of 1985. Ed Bean reported on Thomas Stanley, a marketing professor at Georgia State University in Atlanta, who had been studying "the ways of the rich, particularly those with a net worth of at least $1,000,000, for the past 12 years." What he found, among other things, was that millionaires usually drive "four-door American sedans or Volvos with no chrome. Old station wagons are not uncommon. 'These are the most traditional people in the world,' says Mr. Stanley."

How did they become wealthy? In part by avoiding the most common mistakes individuals make: having a consumptive lifestyle, not having a budget, buying an automobile through financing, and funding a consumptive lifestyle through debt.

Mistake #4: The Debt Trap

At risk of sounding like a broken record, I must again address the liabilities of debt. The common mistakes in financial planning are all, in one way or another, related to debt. Debt and lifestyle go hand in hand in American society. When you use debt to fund a consumptive lifestyle, not only do you have the consumptive lifestyle working against you financially, but you also have the additional burden of the debt working against you financially. Both should be avoided like the plague!

The only absolute way to avoid the use of debt, in the first place, is to have a financial plan prepared at the beginning of each year that does not allow for the use of debt.

The major problem most people face is how to get out of the debt that they are already in. There are only two ways to get out of debt after making the decision to avoid getting further into debt: (1) Examine the assets you have to see which ones could be sold in order to reduce debt; (2) in the absence of assets to sell to eliminate debt, set up a repayment schedule and strictly adhere to it.

I once purchased a used car from a young woman who was in the process of getting a divorce from her husband. During a test drive of the car she told me that the payments on her car, which was less than a year old, were $476 per month. This amount did not include the insurance and other ancillary costs of operation. I don't know what her annual earnings were, but $476 a month had to be a substantial portion of her monthly earnings.

She had purchased the car less than a year earlier and was now having to sell it to me for approximately two-thirds of the purchase price. In doing so, she was freeing up $476 a month or $5,712 per year in cash flow. Obviously, she will have to purchase another car, so that amount is not totally free; but she had reduced her debt by selling the assets that caused the debt.

Other assets that may be sold are investment assets, the liquidation of saving accounts, and perhaps even borrowing from the cash value of life insurance at lower interest rate than what is being paid on credit card and consumer debt.

In determining which assets to sell in order to reduce debt, remember that the assets sold should have a lower yield or appreciation rate than the debt cost.

For example, look back at Bob and Laura's Debt Repayment Worksheet (see page 68). If they sell the boat in order to reduce debt, they should be able to realize $6,000, which is the listed market value on their net worth statement, and of course this $6,000 is generating no income or appreciation. In fact, it is *depreciating*. They could then use the proceeds of that sale to eliminate the boat loan of $5,000, costing $200 per month of cash flow, and save a 14 percent interest rate—not a bad rate of return for any investment. By eliminating the boat loan through the sale of the boat, they essentially made an investment that yielded 14 percent. They also could borrow $1,000 from their life insurance cash value.

If they sell this asset, they will eliminate all of their monthly payments, except the home mortgage, and free up $7,800 on an annual basis, or $650 on a monthly basis, which goes to reduce the negative cash flow margin they have been facing. That $7,800 plus the $5,006 generated by reducing living expenses totals a $12,806 cash flow increase.

However, some of their income is going to disappear from the real estate investment. That amount is $2,150, so the positive cash flow impact of selling assets to reduce debt is $5,650 before considering the tax ramifications of so doing.

The logical questions that come up when considering these actions are twofold. First of all, does selling assets to reduce debt make economic sense? Second, what impact does it have on their tax situation?

First of all, economically they have reduced high cost debt by choosing to sell low-productive or nonproductive assets. Therefore, it will make economic sense over time. The impact on their cash flow is immediately a positive $5,650; the impact on their net worth is neutral. There is no impact on the net worth because a dollar reduction in assets is offset by a dollar reduction in debt.

In Week Eight we will look at the impact of these decisions on their tax planning. For now suffice it to say, it does make tax sense. But even if it did not, the decision would still have been a good one. Why? They have relieved the pressure of continually funding a negative cash flow and enduring the anxiety and strain such a situation causes in a marriage.

Repayment the Hard Way

Not everyone has the luxury, however, of selling assets to repay debt. Many are deeply in debt with virtually no assets at all. In fact, as I've said before, 80 percent of Americans owe more than they own. Selling assets may not be an option. Other than receiving an inheritance or striking oil, the only other option is the slow, painful, and difficult process of making monthly payments. You must decide, first of all, not to take on any more debt, and, second, to set up a schedule of debt repayment.

I recommend that, rather than a debt consolidation loan, you go directly to your creditor with the schedule in hand of how you are going to repay the debt, and that you do two things:

1. Pay something on each debt each month so that the creditor knows you are serious.
2. Concentrate on eliminating the smallest debt first. You need to have some reward quickly for a difficult project. When you have eliminated the smallest debt first, then you can apply the additional amount available from not having to pay on that debt anymore, to the second smallest debt that you have. You will be building momentum that is exciting and encouraging.

One other key to repaying debt is to precommit any extra income—in other words, excess cash flow—to debt payment. This is an opportunity for you to see God working in your financial life. He will provide funds in unexpected and supernatural ways as a result of your obedience to Him. Remember, "You can't eat an elephant in one bite, but you can eat an elephant one bite at a time."

A Time to Reflect

As you have read through these common mistakes, you have undoubtedly been thinking about your situation. Spend some time reflecting on what direction and/or decisions you think God might be leading you to make. Spiritually, what you need to be asking during this time is, "God, what would You have me learn?" not, "God, why am I in this situation?" Chances are good that God did not force you into debt, but by His mercy He will enable you to climb out of your situation.

Have you recently made a major purchase you now regret?

_____

_____

_____

_____

_____

_____

_____

What are your thoughts regarding changes you might make in your lifestyle that would postively impact your financial situation?

_____

_____

_____

_____

_____

_____

_____

_____

_____

Spend some time with your family holding a "brainstorming" session on the subject of living a nonconsumptive lifestyle. Explain your financial situation in simple, yet honest terms, then ask for each family member to think about ways they could begin making nonconsumptive changes. Remember, this is not a time of commitment, this is a time for brainstorming. No idea is too outlandish or silly. Value each person's contribution and respond respectfully to any suggestion. Brainstorming sessions thrive on humor—this is a time to have fun as a family. Go for it! Record all ideas, silly or not. Something creative might come from the silliest of suggestions. Remember, out of the mouths of babes . . .

_____

_____

_____

_____

_____

_____

_____

_____

_____

_____

_____

_____

_____

A Question of Priorities

I am often asked whether couples in a heavy debt situation should tithe or not, and I have two thoughts regarding this. First of all, tithing is no more or less spiritual than debt repayment if God owns it all. However, because God does own it all, a tithe, as a priority, is a statement of your recognition that God owns it all. In other words, I don't believe it is a yes/no question; rather it is a question relative to the individual and the circumstances. A person must, however, bear in mind the two principles: God owns it all and, as a priority, giving is commanded in the Bible. The question of whether to use tithe money to fund debt repayment is a very serious spiritual decision that can only be made with much prayer and godly counsel.

Remember, faith requires a first step without full understanding and without seeing how it is all going to work out. Getting out of debt requires elements very typical of the faith walk. In most cases, for the Christian it requires faith even to take the first step.

Go with the Green

Many years ago when I began thinking of financial planning as a career, I became convinced of the importance of living on a budget. I used credit cards for convenience while I lived according to a budget. Credit cards just made record keeping easier, and because I paid the credit card statements in full each month, there was no interest cost associated with using the credit cards. Then I read somewhere that the *mere use of credit cards will cause a family to spend 34 percent more,* regardless of whether the full statement is paid off each month or not. I found that totally unbelievable and decided to spend a year trying to disprove it.

The only way to disprove the information was not to use credit cards and to go on a straight cash system. So my wife and I put away our credit cards and lived strictly on cash. We paid cash for everything.

By using cash exclusively, my spending mentality changed. It was much more difficult to pay twenty-five dollars for a tank of gas using cash than if I used a credit card. (I still had that Olds 98, affectionately labeled "Old Blue.") Paying cash at the drugstore caused me (at the very least) to hesitate, and in most cases, to eliminate those impulsive purchases at the checkout counter. Paying cash for clothes caused me to think very seriously about each item. Paying cash for car repairs caused me to examine whether it could be done less expensively, either by myself or at another place. Paying cash for airplane tickets while traveling caused me to think a second time about the trip I was taking.

After a year, without using credit cards at all, our living expenses decreased by 33 percent from a level I had thought was "bare bones" to begin with.

Go with the green, at least for a year, until your spending habits are adjusted and you have a set budget based upon a cash level rather than a credit-card level.

Ban the Cards

Giving up credit cards for many people is something akin to going through "withdrawal." First of all, pray about it! Is God leading you to "go cold turkey"? If you can't yet bring yourself to cutting up your credit cards, begin by putting them away somewhere: place them in a gallon container of water and deep freeze them; put them in a bank safety deposit box; or give them to a friend who will hold you accountable. Then make a commitment to yourself, your spouse, or your financial planning partner.

I, _____ , do hereby forfeit my sense of "entitlement" to credit. Today, (Date)_____ , I commit myself to living responsibly within my means and will faithfully work at reducing my dependence on debt. *I will wait at least twenty-four hours before making any purchase,* even if I see something I "have to have." And for a minimum of ninety days, I will go with the green, making "cash only" my policy.

When I've made this recommendation in my seminars, I'm always asked several questions, which may also be troubling you. You may be wondering:

Isn't there a risk in carrying cash?

Of course there is. However, the risk of overspending without planning to pay cash is greater than the loss of cash out of a purse or wallet. The other advantage is that using "cash only" requires planning; in other words, unplanned expenditures are minimized. You learn to plan ahead for the need for cash and be more cautious.

Don't I need my credit cards to establish credit?

Most people have *more* than enough credit *already* established; that's not the problem. However, in many cases a retailer may ask to see a credit card before accepting a check, but often a driver's license will do. This kind of situation offers a tremendous opportunity to share why you don't use credit cards and how God is faithful to provide for you.

Isn't this recommendation awfully restrictive and narrow-minded?

To answer this question, I suggest you reflect on the following verses from Proverbs:

Dishonest money dwindles away,
but he who gathers money little by little makes it grow.
                                        —Proverbs 13:11 NIV

He who has a slack hand becomes poor,
But the hand of the diligent makes rich.
                                        —Proverbs 10:4

The hand of the diligent will rule,
But the lazy man will be put to forced labor.
                                        —Proverbs 12:24

The lazy man does not roast what he took in hunting,
But diligence is a man's precious possession.
                                        —Proverbs 12:27

Poverty and shame will come to him who disdains correction,
But he who regards a rebuke will be honored.
                                        —Proverbs 13:18

The next time you make a spontaneous purchase, ask yourself, What does this really cost me? Likewise, losses on investments or mistakes on major purchases, such as cars, cost far more than it appears because not only must the loss be made up but also what that loss would have earned in the intervening time must be made up.

Keeping a Daily Cash Diary

For the next week, keep a small notebook in your wallet or purse. Keep a running diary of every purchase you make, even if you spend less than a dollar to buy a soda or a cup of coffee. At the end of the week, total your expenditures. Remember, $2.74 spent daily over a year's time on nonproductive items results in an overspending of $1,000 a year. This exercise will simply sensitize you to your level of impulse spending.

GUARANTEED FINANCIAL SUCCESS

You are now ready to prioritize your goals and move on to the "perspiration point" of financial planning. Before next week's session, let's review what you've accomplished. Through the *Master Your Money* financial-planning process you have:

- Gained an understanding of the biblical principles of financial planning.
- Learned the value of a nonconsumptive lifestyle.
- Seen the downfall of debt.
- Begun to set long-term goals.

These represent the three principles of guaranteed financial success:

1. Spend less than you earn over a long period of time.
2. Recognize the opportunity cost of consumption.
3. Avoid costly mistakes.

WEEK SIX

Getting There from Here

Designing a Personal Financial Plan

"The average person's goal these days is to be able to afford what he is spending."

"I can't live on what I'm earning. I can't even live on what I'm spending."

My daughters have grown up hearing me preach money management principles. I reluctantly admit they have wearied of hearing me say, "Do you realize what that is going to cost you at the end of forty years?" On one occasion my daughter Karen was going to do something that was quite obviously a mistake (a father's objective observation, of course!).

"Karen, that's really a silly mistake you're getting ready to make," I told her with all of my fatherly wisdom and tact. "Do you realize what that's going to cost you in forty years?"

"Daddy, do you know how much *no fun* compounded over forty years is?" came her reply without a moment's hesitation.

Her point was well taken. I'm not saying that you save everything that comes into your hands. There is a balance in the Christian life. That balance is what prioritizing your goals and planning your cash flow are all about.

Most of us spend our income, forgetting about tithing, taxes, and saving—priorities more important than lifestyle.

During the last five weeks, you have done a great deal of financial homework. You have:

- Determined your net worth;
- Summarized your cash flow;
- Determined your level of debt and living expenses;
- Put your goals in writing.

You're now ready to prioritize those goals, develop your plan, and put the plan into action. Believe it or not, you're more than halfway there!

Before moving ahead, let me offer one word of encouragement. If you find yourself disturbed by your level of debt—no matter what your level of indebtedness—you will find a way out. By faithfully, honestly addressing your situation, you are doing what God would ask of you. Setting your goals and faithfully following your plan is your part; providing the resources is God's part.

PRIORITIZING YOUR GOALS

Go back and review your Vision of the Future on pages 98–101.

Set priorities for accomplishing these goals by listing them in order on the chart that follows. Once you have prioritized your goals, you have the foundation necessary for determining how much to increase your cash-flow margin and how that margin will be used.

Let me remind you that your goals are faith goals, and by definition:

- You may not be able to see how it will happen;
- You may not have adequate resources.

Although setting goals is your part and providing the resources is God's part, I've found that many of my clients have difficulty "letting go and letting God." If you have followed the process of spending time with God, seeking His will, recording your impressions, defining the goal in measurable terms, all you are called to do is take the first step. Use the following exercise to prioritize your goals, and identify the first step.

Your Faith Goals

We/I believe God wants us to accomplish these specific financial goals this year (by _____):

Priority	Financial Goal	Faith Barrier	My Part (Action Step)	God's Part (Area of Trust)
1	_____	_____	_____	_____
2	_____	_____	_____	_____
3	_____	_____	_____	_____
4	_____	_____	_____	_____
5	_____	_____	_____	_____

For example: One financial goal might be to establish a college fund for your children. The faith barrier is feeling that there is not enough time to save an adequate amount. My part (action step) is to open a savings account for this purpose and to adjust my budget to free up what I can. God's part (area of trust) is to provide the resources to make up the difference.

INCREASING YOUR MARGIN

If you again review the Financial Planning Diagram (page 33), you will see that there are four basic steps to financial planning:

1. Summarize present position;
2. Establish financial goals;
3. Increase cash-flow margin;
4. Control cash flow.

By now I am confident you realize the absolute necessity of increasing your cash-flow margin. And I've emphasized both the spiritual and financial reasons why increasing your cash-flow margin must come primarily from your living expenses and debt reduction. You now have some important decision-making to do regarding your financial plan.

Before looking at your situation, you may find it helpful to see how Bob and Laura approached their cash-flow situation.

The summary (see Increasing Your Margin, pages 132–133) of all the decisions they made is a net increase in cash flow of $6,846. It came from reducing their living expenses by $5,006; reducing their debt by $5,400 through the sale of assets; reducing their tax withholding by $1,000 (this will be explained in Week Eight); and decreasing their investment income through the sale of certain assets.

Bob & Laura
Increasing Your Margin

	MONTHLY AMOUNT	ANNUAL AMOUNT
REDUCE LIVING EXPENSES BY:		
Reduce housing by:	$100	$1,200
Reduce food by:	25	300
Reduce transportation by:	50	600
Reduce entertainment/recreation by:	20	240
Reduce insurance by:		786
Reduce spending on the children by:	90	1,080
Reduce gifts by:		500
Reduce miscellaneous by:	25	300
Total	**$310**	**$5,006**
REDUCE TOTAL DEBT BY:		
Sell boat	$200	$2,400
Borrow $1,000 from insurance		
Sell real estate	200	2,400
Pay off credit cards	50	600
Total	**$450**	**$5,400**
REDUCE TAXES BY:		
Change W-4 to reduce withholding by $1,000		$1,000
Total		**$1,000**
RESTRUCTURE TOTAL INVESTMENTS BY:		
Sell real estate		(2,000)
Total		**(2,000)**

Margin Increase			$9,406
Increase in Giving			(2,560)
TOTAL MARGIN INCREASE			$6,846

Those action steps are then summarized in an analysis of their cash flow, both before planning and after planning as depicted in the Cash-Flow Analysis Summary (pages 133 and 134). Their financial plan is comprised of the action steps taken in the right-hand column and is literally the "After Planning" summary of their cash inflows and cash outflows.

Bob & Laura's
Cash-Flow Analysis Summary

	Before Planning	After Planning	Action Steps
INCOME:	$49,600	$47,600	
LESS:			
Giving	2,200	4,760	
Taxes	10,014	9,014	Increase withholding allowances and reduce amount withheld.
Debt	8,556	3,156	Sell assets and pay off debt except mortgage and car.
Total priority expenses	20,770	16,930	
Net spendable income	$28,830	30,670	
EXPENSES—LIVING:			
Housing	$12,608	$11,408	Reduce by $100/month.
Food	4,800	4,500	Reduce $25/month.
Clothing	1,000	1,000	

Transportation	2,660	2,060	Reduce $50/month by shopping for auto insurance; do maintenance at home.
Entertainment/ Recreation	2,140	1,900	Reduce $20/month.
Medical	1,260	1,260	
Insurance	1,536	750	Cancel policies with debt; replace with $100,000 term insurance.
Children	6,960	$ 5,800	Reduce $90/month.
Gifts	1,150	650	Make some gifts; plan ahead; shop sales.
Miscellaneous	1,380	1,080	Reduce $25/month.
Total	$35,494	$30,488	Options: Increase giving; start college fund; set aside for auto.
Cash-Flow Margin	($6,664)	$ 182	

Notice that they have a net positive cash flow of $182 compared to a preplanning negative cash flow of $6,664. They have done nothing more than decide to go from a negative cash flow to a positive cash flow by adopting a less consumptive lifestyle and by choosing to eliminate their debt by selling assets. Now that they are generating a cash flow margin, Bob and Laura can begin to accomplish their long-term goals.

In reality, their final financial plan will probably have one more element, since they must decide what to do with the positive cash flow margin of $182. Their plan is certainly not comfortable, since there is very little margin for error. However, it is far better than their previous financial situation.

The plan they now have represents the reality of their financial situation. Basically, they could not afford the lifestyle they had adopted, and they were violating a biblical principle by presuming upon the future through the acquisition of debt, probably assuming that they were going to have an increasing income with which to pay off the debt.

Now that their financial plan is in place, we will evaluate it in light of two considerations. First, what is its impact on their personal balance sheet? This one summary statement measures whether a person is making progress or not. The Personal Balance Sheet Analysis Summary is a comparison of their balance sheet before and after planning.

Bob & Laura's
Personal Balance Sheet Analysis Summary

ASSETS:	Before Planning	After Planning	Action Steps
Cash	$ 2,000	$ 2,000	Invest in money market fund.
Savings	1,000	1,500	Cash from sale of assets
Marketable Securities	-0-	-0-	
Life Insurance			Borrow cash value,
Cash Values	6,000	-0-	cancel policies with loans.
Home	112,000	112,000	
Boat	6,000	-0-	Sell and pay off debt.
Automobile	8,000	8,000	
Furniture	5,000	5,000	
Real Estate			
Investments	15,000	-0-	Sell and pay off debt.
Total Assets	$155,000	$128,500	

LIABILITIES:			
Charge Cards	$ 3,000	-0-	
Installment Loans	-0-	-0-	
Auto Loans	6,000	6,000	
Debt to Relatives	5,000	5,000	
Mortgage	81,500	81,500	
Boat Loan	5,000	-0-	
Bank Loans	13,500	-0-	
Life Insurance Plan	5,000	-0-	
Total	$119,000	$ 92,500	
Net Worth	$ 36,000	$ 36,000	

The primary thing to notice is that their net worth did not change, even though they sold $27,000 of investments and assets in order to reduce debt. Basically, they had accumulated assets beyond their ability to accumulate. Therefore, they chose to sell the assets they could not afford in order to pay the debt. This, in turn, increased their cash-flow situation to such an extent that they are now in a much stronger financial position than they were before.

The plan must also be evaluated by a second consideration. Does the personal financial plan move Bob and Laura toward the achievement of their long-term goals?

In light of their goals in the giving area, they have increased their giving to a 10 percent tithe, and they could also choose to give $2,000 for the new chapel at their church by taking the money out of their checking and/or savings account. Of course, that would mean giving up the emergency fund and flexibility factor in their financial situation, but that is not to say it would not be a wise spiritual decision. The decision depends upon the prayerfully set goals that God has given them. At least now, whatever financial decisions they make, they can measure the impact on their situation.

They are not making progress toward the goal of funding college education except to the extent that they can generate a positive cash flow. As they do, the funds can be allocated to this high-priority goal.

A cash-flow margin will also make it possible for Bob and Laura to achieve some of their major lifestyle desires such as replacing Laura's car, and they may choose to use savings account balances or checking account balances to accomplish some of these objectives. The reductions in their living expenses, especially in areas such as entertainment and gifts, may make them feel they are giving up one goal, that of maintaining their present lifestyle, in order to accomplish their other goals. However, my evaluation is that their lifestyle will not be appreciably reduced.

One of their major objectives is to pay off debt. Under this financial plan all their debt will be paid for, with the exception of the home mortgage and the car debt. This is probably the most significant achievement over the long term.

They also indicated they would like to have $5,000 invested in a money-market fund. This is one of the action steps that they can—and should—take as a part of their financial plan. In addition, they would like to pass on to their children at least $100,000. Their net worth of $36,000 is a step toward the accomplishment of that goal and has not been reduced by the financial plan they are putting into place.

The only thing for Bob and Laura to do at this point is to take the action steps they have decided on. Until they do so, they have not exercised faith, for faith without works is dead. Faith always requires action. Once the action steps have been taken and the financial plan is in place and working, they will need to control their living expenses, which is the fourth step of the financial-planning process.

Again, I want to emphasize that financial planning is a process. Circumstances will change throughout the year, goals will change, and desires will change. We live in a dynamic environment and flexibility is one aspect of a financial plan. I recommend that you review your financial plan at least on an annual basis and, in the earlier years of developing the discipline of financial planning, review and perhaps revise your plan on a quarterly basis.

As time goes on, you will find that the process of financial planning becomes almost automatic as you put the principles into practice.

Use the following pages to design your own financial plan and evaluate its impact on your balance sheet. We are now at the "perspiration point" of financial planning. However, it is also the most exciting point, because you can discover the action steps needed to achieve your real goals and to incorporate biblical principles into your daily life.

FINDING MONEY YOU NEVER KNEW YOU HAD

The major key to success in reducing living expenses is recognizing that every dollar saved in the living-expense category goes directly to the cash-flow margin. To evaluate your expenditures, look at each living expense item, line by line, asking yourself if a reduction in that area is possible.

James 1:5 says, "If any of you lacks wisdom, let him ask of God, who gives to all liberally and without reproach." God will give you creative ways to reduce your expenses when you come to Him humbly asking for His guidance and wisdom. It has been my experience that God gives unusual creativity to those who demonstrate a desire and obedience to His plans and purposes. I'll offer a few suggestions and observations regarding your decisions in these areas:[1]

---

[1]Condensed from articles by C. Scott Houser of Ronald Blue & Co., which appeared in the *Master Your Money Newsletter,* available from Ronald Blue & Co., and from the hardback book, *Master Your Money,* published by Thomas Nelson.

1. *Be realistic*. Some areas are not cut at all because there is no ability and/or desire to cut in that area. For example, in Bob and Laura's case, medical expenses and clothing.

2. *Reduce rather than eliminate*. Many of the specific reductions come from foregoing a desired consumption or purchase, such as eliminating eating out one night per month.

3. *Comparison shop*. Some items undoubtedly can be cut by merely shopping better or buying more wisely, such as in the area of insurance.

4. *Be faithful, not foolish*. Be careful not to reduce or eliminate an expense this year that would be more costly at a later time. This is especially true in the areas of maintenance and repairs on automobiles and homes.

5. *Rent rather than buy*. Some things you just don't need to own: vacation homes or cabins, timesharing arrangements, boats, major tools, high-ticket sporting equipment, etc. It's easy and comparatively inexpensive to rent state-of-the-art equipment, return it when you want, and avoid maintenance, depreciation, obsolescence, property taxes, and so on.

6. *Buy used goods*. Contrary to popular belief, buying used goods is not risky and does not take a lot of expertise. It does take planning and research. If at all possible, anticipate your need. If you know you will need a major appliance or a car, begin shopping three or four months before replacement becomes necessary. Consider buying used automobiles, televisions, stereo equipment, refrigerators, freezers, furniture, children's clothing, and tools. Two tips for buying a used car: (1) have a mechanic check it out, and (2) buy only from someone who can produce service records and who you feel has taken good care of his/her car.

7. *Negotiate*. "You have not because you ask not." Don't feel bad about asking a salesman if he or she will take less for an item. Don't pressure; simply ask if that is their best price. The results can be amazing.

8. *Set up a babysitting co-op*. Get together with other couples you know and develop a babysitting plan, trading time on a child-per-child basis. Some co-ops use exchange coupons or poker chips (God can use any man-made object for His purposes!). These can be convenient means of payment, and save you a significant amount of money.

9. *Stock up on gifts*. For birthdays, showers, and Christmas gifts, consider stocking up on presents by buying items on sale or at the end of the

season and storing them until needed. Christmas comes at the same time every year; plan ahead and avoid the temptation to pull out those plastic cards at the last minute.

10. *Stockpile anticipated needs*. If possible, buy products in quantity—canned or dried foods, paper goods, etc. Shop clearance sales, membership warehouses, or other special sales.

Increasing Your Margin

	MONTHLY AMOUNT	ANNUAL AMOUNT
REDUCE LIVING EXPENSES BY:		
Reduce housing by:	_____	_____
Reduce food by:	_____	_____
Reduce transportation by:	_____	_____
Reduce entertainment/recreation by:	_____	_____
Reduce insurance by:	_____	_____
Reduce spending on the children by:	_____	_____
Reduce gifts by:	_____	_____
Reduce miscellaneous by:	_____	_____
Total	_____	_____

REDUCE TOTAL DEBT BY:

_____
_____
_____

| **Total** | _____ | _____ |

REDUCE TAXES BY:

_____
_____
_____

| **Total** | _____ | _____ |

RESTRUCTURE TOTAL INVESTMENTS BY:

_____

_____

Total _____ _____

Margin Increase _____ _____

Increase in Giving _____ _____

TOTAL MARGIN INCREASE _____ _____

Your Cash-Flow Analysis Summary

	Before Planning	After Planning	Action Steps
INCOME:			
LESS:			
Giving	_____	_____	_____
Taxes	_____	_____	_____
Debt	_____	_____	_____
Total priority expenses	_____	_____	_____
Net spendable income	_____	_____	_____
EXPENSES—LIVING:			
Housing	_____	_____	_____
Food	_____	_____	_____
Clothing	_____	_____	_____
Transportation	_____	_____	
Entertainment/ recreation	_____	_____	_____
Medical	_____	_____	_____
Insurance	_____	_____	_____
Children	_____	_____	_____
Gifts	_____	_____	_____
Miscellaneous	_____	_____	_____
Total	_____	_____	_____
Cash-Flow Margin	_____	_____	_____

Your Personal Balance Sheet Analysis Summary

ASSETS:	Before Planning	After Planning	Action Steps
_____	_____	_____	_____
_____	_____	_____	_____
_____	_____	_____	_____
_____	_____	_____	_____
_____	_____	_____	_____
_____	_____	_____	_____
_____	_____	_____	_____
_____	_____	_____	_____
_____	_____	_____	_____
_____	_____	_____	_____
Total Assets	_____	_____	

LIABILITIES:

	Before Planning	After Planning	Action Steps
_____	_____	_____	_____
_____	_____	_____	_____
_____	_____	_____	_____
_____	_____	_____	_____
_____	_____	_____	_____
_____	_____	_____	_____
_____	_____	_____	_____
_____	_____	_____	_____
_____	_____	_____	_____
_____	_____	_____	_____
Total Liabilities	_____	_____	
Net Worth	_____	_____	

WEEK SEVEN
Putting It All Together

Controlling the Cash Flow

"No longer feeling a sense of dread when I sit down to pay the bills is a wonderful feeling," Bob said. "I just wish we had done this financial planning sooner."

One year after initially developing their financial plan, Bob and Laura were virtually debt-free. The motivation to stick to their plan came from Bob's determination to go into business for himself. The compromise they reached was this:

- Bob promised Laura he would not apply for a credit line to fund going into business for himself, until they had completed the *Master Your Money* financial-planning process.
- With their financial planning in order, Laura agreed to support Bob in his desire to eventually leave his current job to go on his own.

However, Laura was right when she told Bob, "We're broke." With all their financial affairs in order, all the homework completed, all the facts and figures in place, Bob was ready to meet with a loan officer to apply for a credit line to fund his first year in business. Did he get the funding? No. The credit line was denied. The reason? They had too much debt. So they went to work, and eighteen months later, their hands were no longer tied by a 77 percent propensity to borrow. Surprisingly, once they were in a healthy financial position, Bob had changed his mind. Financial freedom felt pretty good.

"A year and a half later, I was all ready to go back to the banker," Bob told me. "But something had changed. I looked at things differently. Words from the planning process kept coming back to me. 'Debt always mortgages the future.' 'On the front end, every business and investment deal looks like a good one.' 'Seek God's will and direction.'

"I realized working for myself was no longer that important to me at this time in my life. Someday, maybe. But Laura and I feel like God is calling us in another direction for now."

What Bob and Laura accomplished, you will too. Controlling their cash flow, lowering their debt, and living within a budget is the ticket to financial peace of mind. Bob and Laura turned their financial situation around in a fairly short period of time. You may find it will take you two, three, even five years to work your way out of debt and into financial health. I've said several times and will say again, *financial planning is a process*. The key to your success is simple: *Work the plan, and trust the process*. After all, God owns it all. God is in control.

CONTROL THE FLOW

Reducing your spending is not unlike reducing your calories. Weight-loss professionals will tell you that diets don't work. Weight is lost, but quickly regained. The only effective way to lose weight is to make long-term changes in your eating patterns. So too with spending patterns. A budget mentality is one of short-term constraints, a deprivation mentality. A cash-control system is not restrictive, but rather freeing. A cash-control system is planned spending, not restricted spending. Once your cash-control system is in place, you really don't care about being a little bit over or under in each category. You're spending according to a plan, and over time, you'll be surprised at the progress you will be making toward your financial goals. Remember: *Work the plan, and trust the process*.

We've all heard stories about the cookie jar where Grandpa and Grandma used to keep all their cash. When money was earned, it went into the cookie jar. As needs arose, the money to pay for them was taken out of the cookie jar. When the cookie jar was empty, there was no more spending until more cash was received.

As time went on and the management of expenses became more complex, many of our grandparents gave up the cookie jar and went to an envelope system. Money was placed in various envelopes according to the allocations of the income—one envelope for food, one envelope for clothes, one envelope for giving . . . The income was placed into the envelopes, and spent in the various areas allotted. When an envelope was empty, spending in that category stopped until more cash was received and placed in the envelope.

The cookie jar or envelope system demonstrates three basic principles of cash-flow control.

1. The money was always preallocated.
2. Spending always stopped when the envelope or cookie jar was empty.
3. The individuals always had a current awareness of the cash available relative to their planned expenditures.

In other words, with envelope allocations it was very simple to determine whether any money was left.

These same principles form the basis for any cash-control system:

1. A preallocation of income;
2. An end to spending when the spending limit is reached;
3. A current awareness of the financial situation relative to the plan.

A CASH-FLOW PLAN

You will develop your cash flow plan through five steps:

1. Estimate your living expenses.
2. Find out what you are actually spending.
3. Establish spending allocations.
4. Implement a cash control system.
5. Evaluate and revise.

Your cash-flow plan may take you as long as two years to put in place. A cash-flow plan is never the law, but rather a guide. For the plan to work, *it is essential that you be flexible* (and forgiving!).

Step 1: Estimate Your Living Expenses

Go back to your Living Expenses Worksheet on pages 76–78. Transfer your estimates for each category to the Living Expenses Worksheet on pages 147–149.

Step 2: Find Out What You Are Actually Spending

Go back through your checkbook ledger for the last six to twelve weeks, recording each expenditure under the appropriate category in the ledger provided on page 146. You will now be able to compare your actual spending with your estimations. A Living Expenses Worksheet is provided for you to compare your estimated expenses to your actual expenses when you complete your checkbook inventory. Figure your living expenses on an annual basis. In other words, if you analyze four weeks of your checkbook, multiply the total amount by twelve to get your annual amount. If you go through three months of your checkbook, multiply by four. The point is to get an annual projection. (You can also do this on your computer with a compatible software program. This may be the opportunity you've been looking for to justify that personal computer expense—*but don't borrow, charge, or finance it!*).

Remember: Shoot for 80 percent accuracy!

If you have frequent automatic-teller withdrawals for cash, and are unable to remember what the cash was used for, I suggest you keep an ATM expenditure diary for a few weeks to see what kinds of expenses you are spending the cash on. Then, make appropriate changes in your Living Expenses Inventory. Otherwise, make estimates of what types of expenses the ATM withdrawals cover and allocate accordingly.

Rather than analyzing their actual spending retroactively, some people prefer to record their spending by category for the next three months. Recording your actual expenditures will increase your awareness and help you control your spending. One word of caution: Don't put your planning process on hold while you are recording your actual expenditures. Go ahead with the process, estimating by category and reviewing and revising on a regular basis.

Living Expense Inventory

Estimates vs. Actuals

Checkbook Inventory Worksheet

Expense Description	Housing	Food	Clothing	Transportation	Entertainment Recreation	Medical	Insurance	Children	Gifts/Special Occasions	Misc.

Living Expenses

YEAR: _____	Annual Estimate From Wk 3	Annual Actual From Checkbook Inventory	Amount We Will Budget
HOUSING			
Mortgage/rent	_____	_____	_____
Insurance	_____	_____	_____
Property taxes	_____	_____	_____
Electricity	_____	_____	_____
Heating	_____	_____	_____
Water	_____	_____	_____
Sanitation	_____	_____	_____
Telephone	_____	_____	_____
Cleaning	_____	_____	_____
Repairs/maintenance	_____	_____	_____
Improvements	_____	_____	_____
Furnishings	_____	_____	_____
Supplies	_____	_____	_____
Other	_____	_____	_____
Total Housing	_____	_____	_____
FOOD	_____	_____	_____
CLOTHING	_____	_____	_____
Husband	_____	_____	_____
Wife	_____	_____	_____
Children	_____	_____	_____
Total Clothing	_____	_____	_____
TRANSPORTATION	_____	_____	_____
Insurance	_____	_____	_____
Gas & oil	_____	_____	_____
Repairs/maintenance	_____	_____	_____
Parking	_____	_____	_____
Mass transit or commute	_____	_____	_____

YEAR: _____	Annual Estimate From Wk 3	Annual Actual From Checkbook Inventory	Amount We Will Budget
Other	_____	_____	_____
Total Transportation	_____	_____	_____
ENTERTAINMENT/RECREATION	_____	_____	_____
Eating out	_____	_____	_____
Babysitters	_____	_____	_____
Magazines/newspapers/cable	_____	_____	_____
Vacation	_____	_____	_____
Clubs/activities	_____	_____	_____
Classes/courses	_____	_____	_____
Other	_____	_____	_____
Total Entertainment	_____	_____	_____
MEDICAL EXPENSES	_____	_____	_____
Insurance	_____	_____	_____
Doctors	_____	_____	_____
Dentists	_____	_____	_____
Drugs	_____	_____	_____
Total Medical Expenses	_____	_____	_____
INSURANCE	_____	_____	_____
Life	_____	_____	_____
Disability	_____	_____	_____
Other	_____	_____	_____
Total Insurance	_____	_____	_____
CHILDREN	_____	_____	_____
School lunches	_____	_____	_____
Allowances	_____	_____	_____
Tuition	_____	_____	_____
Lessons	_____	_____	_____
Other	_____	_____	_____
Total Children	_____	_____	_____

YEAR: _____	Annual Estimate From Wk 3	Annual Actual From Checkbook Inventory	Amount We Will Budget
GIFTS/SPECIAL OCCASIONS	_____	_____	_____
Christmas	_____	_____	_____
Birthdays	_____	_____	_____
Anniversary	_____	_____	_____
Holidays other than Christmas	_____	_____	_____
Other	_____	_____	_____
Total Gifts	_____	_____	_____
MISCELLANEOUS	_____	_____	_____
Toiletries	_____	_____	_____
Husband: lunches, etc.	_____	_____	_____
Wife: miscellaneous	_____	_____	_____
Dry cleaning/laundry	_____	_____	_____
Animal care	_____	_____	_____
Beauty/barber	_____	_____	_____
Other	_____	_____	_____
Other	_____	_____	_____
Total Miscellaneous	_____	_____	_____
TOTAL LIVING EXPENSES	_____	_____	_____

Step 3: Establish Spending Allocations

Once you have compared your actual spending to your estimated spending, you are ready to establish your spending allocations or budgeted amounts for each category.

You may want to refer to the Percentage Guide on page 150. Again, this is not a rule, but merely a guide to assist you in your planning.

Your Family Income Percentage Guide

All percentages are of gross income.

Gross Income	$20,000	30,000	40,000	50,000	60,000	$	%
Less:							
Giving	10%	10%	10%	10%	10%		
Taxes/S.S.	17%	18%	19%	22%	22%		
Debt	0%	0%	0%	0%	0%		
Total Priority Expenses	27%	28%	29%	32%	32%		
Net Spendable Income	73%	72%	71%	68%	68%		
Living Expenses							
Housing	26%	25%	21%	20%	18%		
Food	15%	12%	4%	7%	7%		
Clothing	4%	4%	4%	4%	3%		
Trans.	10%	7%	6%	5%	5%		
Ent./Rec.	4%	5%	6%	6%	6%		
Medical	2%	2%	2%	2%	2%		
Insurance	1%	2%	2%	2%	2%		
Children	2%	1%	1%	1%	1%		
Gifts	1%	1%	1%	1%	1%		
Misc.	4%	4%	4%	3%	3%		
Total Living Expenses	69%	63%	56%	51%	48%		
Margin	4%	9%	15%	17%	20%		

ASSUMPTIONS:

1. Figures are based on a family of four.
2. The tax deductions are giving, interest on home mortgage, state and city income taxes, and property taxes.
3. Home is owned.
4. There is no debt other than home mortgage.
5. All Social Security withholdings are from one wage earner.
6. Estimates based on 1990 tax schedules and allowable deductions.
7. Margin can be used for other expenses (private education, etc.).

Step 4: Implement a Cash-Control System

In today's environment, it is not often convenient or wise to keep envelopes with cash lying around, although many couples I know still use the basic envelope system to control their spending. Each month they put a pre-allocated amount of money into various envelopes and stop spending when the envelopes are empty. What's most important is to develop a cash-flow control method that works for you.

The system I recommend is one that uses checkbook-style ledgers in place of envelopes. This system adapts the envelope method to work with checking and savings accounts. Using checkbook-style ledgers (the kind used in wallet-size checkbooks available from your bank), each checkbook ledger has the effect of serving as an envelope in the budget system.

You will need to commit to several principles or operating procedures in your cash-flow control system.

1. Assigned accountability. Husband and wife must each have areas of budget responsibility. For example, the husband may be responsible for mortgage and utility payments while the wife is responsible for food and miscellaneous spending. Each is assigned the cash allocations necessary to fulfill these functions.

2. Immediate awareness of how actual spending measures against planned spending. The key is to know as soon as possible when budget limits have been reached.

3. Commitment to consistency. Is controlling cash flow extra work? You bet it is. However, the benefits are more than worth the effort. And once your allocations are established, it should not require more than twenty to thirty minutes during the week. Eventually cash-flow control will require no more than twenty to thirty minutes a month.

4. Strict limitation of credit card use. Nothing will destroy a budget faster than having to meet unexpected debt payments. Use credit cards *only* as a check (a bank debit card makes this more convenient), writing the amount charged into your checkbook at the time of the purchase. Then you will always have the funds to pay the full amount when you receive the bill. Credit is not the problem. The *misuse* of credit—failing to pay the balance in full each month—is what accumulates debt. I will remind you, however, using credit for convenience will more than likely increase your spending by as much as 34 percent over a cash-only policy.

5. *Regular accumulation of all cash-flow margin.* All funds not used during the month are transferred to savings. If spending is being done on an average basis, then it will be necessary during some months to transfer from savings back into the budget.

6. *Be flexible.* At times it may be necessary to use funds allocated for one purpose for some other purpose. This is perfectly normal, but it does require *a specific decision* each time a transfer is made. For example, you may decide to give up entertainment money to buy clothes. Monitoring your cash flow allows this to be done visibly and intentionally. Remember, cash-flow control is by design, not default.

7. *Allocate ahead of time for budget busters.* Every month or every paycheck, some amount should be set aside in a savings or separate checking account for the expenses that will occur on other than a monthly basis and for unexpected expenses. Vacation, gifts, insurance payments, car repairs, and seasonal clothing are all examples of this type of expense. The Fixed Annual Expenses worksheet on pages 152–153 will help you determine what this amount should be.

Bob & Laura's Fixed Annual Expenses

Projected, As of January 1

	When Paid	Annual Amount	Annual Divided by 12	Months Since Paid	Beginning Balance Needed
Home Insurance	8/1	$400	$33	5.0	$165
Property Tax	10/15	1,000	83	2.5	208
Life Insurance					
Medical Insurance					
Disability Insurance					
Auto Insurance	6/1	500	42	7.0	294
Other Insurance					
Other Insurance					
Other Taxes					
Dues: Racquet Club	9/15	300	25	3.5	88
Dues:					

	When Paid	Annual Amount	Annual Divided by 12	Months Since Paid	Beginning Balance Needed
School Tuition	8/1	6,000	500	5.0	2,500
Other: Vacation	7/1	1,000	83	6.0	498
Other: Clothing	Varies	1,000	83		
Other: Gifts	Varies	1,150	96		
Other:					
TOTAL		**$11,350**			**$3,753**
Monthly Payment To Reserve Fund			$945		

An Overview of the Cash-Control System

The Cash Control Overview Diagram on page 154 will give you the sequence of implementing your cash-control plan each month or pay period.

1. All funds are deposited in the checking account.
2. Each deposit is noted in the deposits and allocations ledger.
3. At the specific pay interval, each major ledger is given a deposit according to the allocation schedule. The allocation is noted as a withdrawal from the deposits and allocations ledger.
4. Allocations are noted as deposits in each ledger.
5. Cash is disbursed through the husband's and wife's checkbooks and ledgers. Their spending must be limited to the allocated amounts.
6. As annual expenses are made (or giving or debt payments) a transfer is made from the annual expense ledger to the husband's or wife's ledger and checkbook. The check is then written for the expense.
7. The annual margin should be accounted for in the checking account at the end of the year (or, if you prefer, more frequently as you are initially putting your plan into practice).

Cash-Control Overview

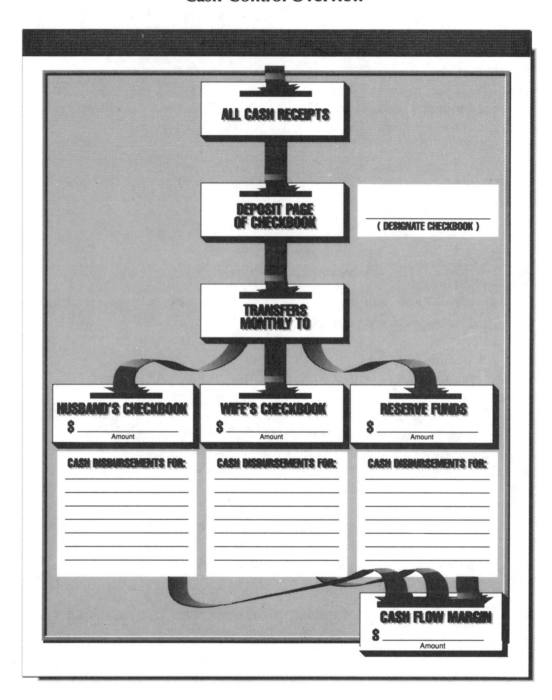

Establish Your Cash-Control System

1. Update the Living Expense Inventory (pages 147–149) to reflect any changes from your checkbook inventory (actual spending versus estimates) and the adjustments made to increase your margins (such as eliminating debt payments if any debts were paid off).
2. Assign the areas of accountability for husband (H) and wife (W).
3. Decide how many ledgers (envelopes) you want to use. You will need at least three:

   • Deposits and allocations;
   • Husband's expenses;
   • Wife's expenses.
   You may want to add:
   • Annual expenses;
   • Giving;
   • Debts;
   • Taxes (if you are self-employed).

4. You are ready to implement your cash-control system.

Ledger Illustration

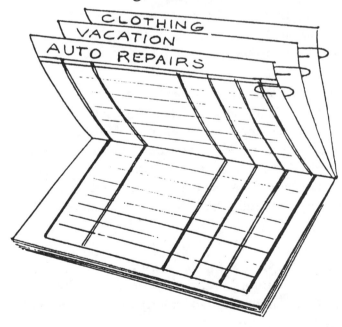

Questions and Answers on Cash Control

How many ledgers can I have?

All you want. But remember, the more ledgers you have, the more cumbersome the system becomes. You may want to start with several to make sure you have control of each area of spending. As you get familiar with how it works, and disciplined to living within your allocations, you may want to simplify by combining several ledgers into one.

The overall admonition is: KEEP IT SIMPLE.

How do I balance my checkbook with all these ledgers and both husband and wife writing checks?

It is really no different from balancing with one checkbook except that the balances in the different ledgers must be considered. Deposits would have to be reconciled with the Deposits and Allocations Ledger. Each cancelled check would have to be reconciled with the husband's or wife's checkbook just as you would normally do with one checkbook.

What if I use a credit card for a purchase?

Transfer funds from the appropriate ledger into the debt ledger. Then the funds will be available to pay the bill when it arrives and you avoid interest charges. If the funds are not available to transfer to the debt ledger, then this is a wrong use of credit cards.

What if I make a purchase with a debit card?

A debit card is used just as a credit card is used, however, the transaction is treated the same as writing a check. Instead of being billed for the purchase, the purchase amount will be deducted from your checking account. Since it is the same as a check, an entry for this amount should be made in your check ledger as soon as possible. A debit card is a good cash control tool and is recommended over the credit card. VISA and MasterCard banks can supply debit cards.

Can I use my margin for special purchases?

You can use the margin for any purpose you desire. Remember that the reason for generating margin is to meet long-range goals and priorities. If you use the margin today you give up the opportunity to meet long-range goals tomorrow.

I am paid on a commission-only basis so my income is variable. How do I handle this?

Keep in mind that only a fixed amount of money is allocated to living expenses each month. All funds are deposited into the checking account and accounted for in the Deposits and Allocations Ledger. In high commission periods a surplus should develop, which should supply funds during low (or no) commission periods. Obviously the best way to start the budget is during a high (income greater than expenses) period. If this is not possible, then it may be necessary to delay allocating funds to annual expenses and concentrate on allocating only for present living expenses until commissions improve.

I am self-employed. Will the budget work for me?

It works the same as for employed people and those with variable incomes. You may need an additional ledger to account for self-employment taxes and for federal and state withholding taxes. Each time a deposit is made, then the transfer of an appropriate percentage for taxes should be made to a tax ledger. This is an untouchable ledger, i.e., this money is not available for transfer for any other purpose. If you do not have the discipline to not spend tax money, then open a separate savings account to hold these funds.

I like to keep some cash when I deposit my paycheck. How do I account for this in the budget?

What is the cash for? That is the chief issue. Simply account for any cash kept by reducing the amount transferred from the Deposits and Allocation Ledger to the appropriate ledger. For example, the husband keeps $50 for gasoline and miscellaneous cash. Then he would reduce the amount that is allocated to his checkbook by $50.

I have some annual expenses coming due but do not have the cash available to meet them and *the needed household expenses. How can I start the budget?*

The ideal way to start a budget is to have a lump sum of money available for annual expenses. If we start the budget with $2,000 available, then during the year we would dip into the $2,000. By the end of the year we would have recovered through regular annual expense allocation and still have $2,000.

If you do not have the initial cash, then every time an annual expense comes due, you will have to decide what you are going to give up in order to meet that expense. However, if you keep making annual allocations on a regular basis you will eventually overcome this problem.

I did not see any place in the budget for furniture, home furnishings, improvements, or appliance replacement. Where are these covered?

These are major purchase items and their purchase is made as a discretionary use of margin.

Clothing expense is lumped in with annual expenses. Can I consider this and other items separately?

You can have all the detail you want. There are several ways to do this. You can set up a separate ledger for clothing. This is probably the simplest way. Or you can subdivide any ledger into components. For example, the Annual Expense Allocation Ledger could be divided into clothing, vacation, gifts, auto repair, insurance, taxes, and so on. A way to apply this would be to use page markers within a ledger book to separate the different areas. Paper clips could be used as page markers.

You will need to determine how much of the annual expenses will be allocated to each area and simply make transfers back to husband and wife checkbooks as before.

A monthly allocation for clothing can also be made directly to the husband's or wife's checkbook ledger. If separation were desired, then once again paper clips could be used to mark the applicable pages.

How do I find the cash balance of my checking account?

Add the bottom line of each of the ledgers together. In other words, after allowing for checks, service charges, and deposits not shown on the bank statement, you would use this formula:

    Deposits ledger balance
+ Husband's ledger balance
+ Wife's ledger balance
+ Giving ledger balance
+ Annual expenses ledger balance

= Balance in the checking account

Step 5: Evaluate and Revise

Once you have been operating with a cash-flow control system, you need to evaluate and revise the plan periodically. One of the purposes of generating your financial plan is to decide where you want to go and to know when you have arrived. To make sure you are on the right track, a periodic review is vital. A quarterly review is great and an annual review is minimum.

The purpose of the review is to ask yourself the following questions:

1. Am I staying within the monthly level of spending decided on for our family? If not, why not? What needs to be adjusted?
2. Can I account for the margins I estimated could accrue? Can I check my bank account on a regular basis and see those margins as increased balances?
3. Am I weighing spending decisions against the goals?
4. Is my net worth increasing?
5. Have I reached any goals?
6. Do I need new goals or to revise any goals?
7. Have insurance needs changed?

SET A FINANCIAL REVIEW DATE

Pull out your calendar now and determine the date of your financial review. Write the financial review on both your and your spouse's calendars; if you have a secretary/assistant who schedules your calendar appointments, you might want to make yourself accountable to her/him as well.

At that time, the plan needs to come off the shelf for the purpose of evaluating your goals, margins, and cash-flow control. Use the following checklist for your review session.

FINANCIAL PLAN REVIEW

1. Review written goals.
   a. Have any goals changed?
   b. Are the short-range goals expressed in dollars and time quantities?

2. Update the net worth information to reflect any changes.
   a. Is the net worth growing?
   b. If not, is there a reason?

3. Were the projected margin accumulations met?
   a. If not, can we tell why?
   b. Do living expenses need to be adjusted?
   c. Are any major purchases planned for the coming year?
   d. Are emergency funds adequate?

4. Is the cash-control system working as planned?
   a. Do we need to make adjustments in any area?
   b. Is debt decreasing?

5. Have the margin accumulations been allocated as planned?
   a. Are we setting aside funds for:
   College?
   Retirement?
   Additional giving?
   Paying off debt?

6. Review the insurance situation.
   a. Is the life insurance summary up to date?
   b. Have we experienced a change that would indicate a need to raise or lower insurance coverage?
   c. Is disability insurance adequate?

7. Are our wills adequate and up-to-date?
   a. Do we need to seek advice on estate planning or using trusts?

8. Have all investments been reviewed?
   a. Do we know the rates of return on all investments?
   b. Have IRA's been funded as early in the year as possible?
   c. Are we following the sequential investment strategy?

Growth Strategies and Investment Opportunities

Tax and Investment Planning

Session Comments:

This week's session on tax planning and investment opportunities is more educational than pro-active. You will want to review this information now, yet plan to use this material for reference when considering future decisions. For your immediate financial planning purposes, I recommend you carefully review the Income Tax Analysis worksheet and the Sequential Investment Strategy section on pages 185–188. If you are considering a decision with major tax or investment ramifications, I strongly advise that you seek professional counsel.

If there is one cash outflow that everyone is anxious to reduce, it is income taxes.

Some time ago I had a client in my office who asked me to help him plan to pay zero taxes. He was a professional who earned a very good income, and yet he was adamant that he did not want to pay taxes. He did not agree with the way the government spent his money. I was tempted to ask him whether he would like to give up his automobile—because the road systems would not be maintained without taxes—or whether he could sleep at night with no military forces to protect him, and whether he would like not having national parks to visit.

I am in no way proposing that we should pay more than we rightfully owe in taxes. There is a big difference, however, between tax avoidance and tax evasion. Tax evasion results in a jail sentence; tax avoidance results in lower taxes, but almost never does it result in no taxes. Tax avoidance is planning wisely and prudently to pay a fair share of taxes, but no more than what is rightfully owed.

I have often reflected on our attitude toward taxes and asked myself the question, Why is it that we detest paying taxes? I believe the answer is multi-faceted, but the primary reason is that we get no perceived immediate benefit from paying taxes. Only in this area of our finances do we feel that once the money is gone, it seems to be gone forever. For the salaried and those living on a fixed income, taxes take a disproportionate share of income compared to those who have the opportunity and ability to use various tax planning tools and techniques.

When I was a practicing CPA, I prepared hundreds of tax returns each year, and was asked hundreds of times over the course of several years, "How can I reduce my taxes?" I had a facetious answer for that question: "It's easy to reduce your taxes—just reduce your income." It's a guaranteed way to re-duce taxes, and there is no risk to it. The point is that if your taxes are going up, your income is also going up. Taxes need to be put into proper perspec-tive, and the proper perspective is that income taxes are levied only where there is income earned.

The second guaranteed way to reduce taxes is to spend more money on deductible items, such as charitable contributions, medical bills, interest costs, and professional fees. As I pointed out in an earlier chapter, there is no such thing as a free tax deduction. If you are in the 15 percent tax bracket, then a dollar spent on a deductible item costs you eighty-five cents cash out of pocket. True, it reduces your taxes, but there has been a cost to it. I can state unequivocally that there is no free tax deduction anywhere, at any time, for anything! When you read or hear of persons who pay no taxes or pay low taxes and have huge incomes, that may be true in the short term because of their high deductions, but those deductions have to be paid for at some time. Here is the guiding principle for tax deductions:

Don't ever expect to get a free tax deduction and never make a financial decision on the basis of its tax deductibility.

It's easy for a tax accountant to make the client happy by having him overpay on withholdings and quarterly tax estimates during the year so that he always gets a refund. I don't believe this is ethical, and it certainly does not make good economic sense.

Getting a tax refund check is a sign of poor stewardship.

A refund check means that the tax payer has planned poorly. The United States government does not require anyone to pay tax withholding or quarterly estimates any higher than what the taxpayer has determined the actual liability will be. A refund check is, in almost every case, a sign of poor planning.

I know that the two preceding general principles may be difficult to deal with personally, because they go against the grain of everything you thought, and perhaps even the way you have planned. For example, many people plan to have that refund check in order to make major purchases each year, but what they are really doing is admitting they do not have the discipline to save for that major purchase. Please remember that tax planning does not have to be a mystery or even very difficult, especially if you understand the two principles above.

SCRIPTURAL INSIGHTS ON TAXES

I have been looking in the Bible for the verse that says, "Thou shalt not pay any taxes." Unfortunately, I haven't been able to find it; nor have I been able to find a verse that tells me exactly how much I should pay in income taxes. However, I do find many principles throughout Scripture that directly apply to income taxes. Read the following verses and in the spaces that follow, write what you feel each verse is saying to Christians living in our contemporary society.

Dishonest money dwindles away,
but he who gathers money little by little makes it grow.
                                        —Proverbs 13:11 NIV

_____

_____

_____

_____

He who is faithful in what is least is faithful also in much; and he who is unjust in what is least is unjust also in much.
                                                                    —Luke 16:10

_____

_____

_____

_____

But we have renounced the hidden things of shame, not walking in craftiness nor handling the word of God deceitfully, but by manifestation of the truth commending ourselves to every man's conscience in the sight of God.
                                    —2 Corinthians 4:2 (emphasis mine)

_____

_____

_____

_____

Render therefore to all their due: taxes to whom taxes are due, customs to whom customs, fear to whom fear, honor to whom honor.
                                                                    —Romans 13:7

_____

_____

_____

_____

_____

"Is it lawful for us to pay taxes to Caesar or not?" . . . "Show Me a denarius. Whose image and inscription does it have?" They answered and said, "Caesar's." And He said to them, "Render therefore to Caesar the things that are Caesar's, and to God the things that are God's."
                                         —Luke 20:22, 24–25

_____

_____

_____

_____

_____

Let your light so shine before men, that they may see your good works and glorify your Father in heaven.
                                         —Matthew 5:16

_____

_____

_____

_____

_____

Without counsel, plans go awry,
But in the multitude of counselors they are established.
                                         —Proverbs 15:22

_____

_____

_____

_____

_____

Let's review these biblical insights

- You are called to be salt and light to a dying world. One of the ways that you are salt and light is by your good stewardship, which will require paying taxes.
- Your choice is fraud or faithfulness. You may reduce taxes by illegal or questionable means, but faithfulness requires you to do good planning and honesty to reduce taxes. Your objective is faithfulness—not tax reduction.
- Some taxes are certainly due, because our government has supplied services. Quite frankly, the freedoms and protection we enjoy in the United States are unparalleled anywhere in the world, and I believe that we all have a part in paying for these privileges. (I am not endorsing wastefulness and poor decisions on the part of our government, but the way to change that is through changing our representation in Congress.)
- Be a planner—not a responder. It is especially important to plan in the tax area because of the many types of taxes you have.

TYPES OF TAXES

It has been rightly said that you are taxed when you earn, you are taxed when you spend, you are taxed when you give, you are taxed when your investments do well, and you are taxed when you die. As a matter of fact, you are taxed almost any time there is a money transaction.

Some of the many kinds of taxes that you pay are:

- *Income taxes*—Federal, state, city, and county taxes on income earned.
- *Sales taxes*—Taxes imposed by state and local communities on sales of all types of goods and services.
- *Intangible taxes*—Taxes on various intangible properties owned, usually including stocks, bonds, and other investments. This tax is generally imposed by state governments.
- *Use taxes*—Taxes for the use of goods and services provided by taxing authorities, such as gasoline taxes for the use of roads and airport taxes for the use of airports.
- *Estate taxes*—Taxes imposed by the federal government on the accumulation of material wealth when a person dies.

- *Inheritance taxes*—Taxes imposed by state and local governments, again, on estates accumulated.
- *Gift taxes*—Taxes imposed on the transfer of various kinds of property to another person. Gift taxes and estate taxes are typically referred to as transfer taxes. In other words, the transferring of property from one person to another results in a tax.
- *Property taxes*—Taxes imposed by local authorities on property owned.
- *Social Security taxes*—Taxes imposed by the federal government on wages, earnings, and self-employment income to pay for social security benefits.

This list is not meant to be all-inclusive, but merely to illustrate that you do pay taxes at almost every turn of your financial life. This week I will discuss tax planning in the area of income taxes at the state and federal levels only. When we address estate planning, I will deal with transfer taxes. None of the other taxes will be covered in this book, because they are basically noncontrollable, except as they relate to other spending decisions.

Income Tax Rates

Two terms must be understood before we discuss tax planning: marginal tax rates and effective tax rates or, stated another way, marginal tax brackets and effective tax brackets. When people say they are in a 15 percent tax bracket, they mean that their next dollar of income is taxed at the 15 percent level or, conversely, that their next dollar of tax deduction reduces taxes by fifteen cents.

The graduated income tax system in the United States means that various levels of income are taxed at different rates. As the income reaches a higher level, the rate goes up, but, and this is important to remember, the rate does not go up on all of the previously earned and taxed income—it only applies to that level. For illustrative purposes I have constructed a hypothetical tax table as follows:

To clarify this illustration, let's define some terms.

Taxable Income. Taxable income is the portion of your earned income that is ultimately taxed after taking into account all deductions, exemptions, and other reductions due to investments, IRA's, and the like.

Column 3 gives the tax bracket, which is the percentage applied to all

Chart 12-A
Hypothetical Tax Table

(1) If Taxable Income is	(2) Tax on Column 1	(3) Tax on Excess
$10,000	$ 1,000	12%
20,000	2,200	15%
30,000	3,700	20%
40,000	5,700	30%
50,000	8,700	40%
60,000	12,700	50%

taxable income in excess of Column 1. In other words, if the taxable income in this illustration is between $10,001 and $20,000, the tax bracket is 12 percent. Thus, 12 percent is paid on all taxable income over $10,000.

Marginal Rate. This determines the amount that will be paid on the next dollar of income that cannot be offset with a deduction. If a person currently has taxable income of $30,000 and he earns one more dollar of income, that dollar of income is taxed at 20 percent. Therefore, his marginal rate is 20 percent, and that stays 20 percent until his taxable income reaches $40,001, at which time the marginal rate to be paid goes to 30 percent. The marginal rate and the tax bracket could be the same, but won't always be. The tax bracket is determined by the last dollar of the taxable income, and the marginal rate is determined by the next dollar of taxable income. This bar chart (see page 169) illustrates how the maximum marginal tax rate has changed over time. Note how low the marginal rate is as we enter the 1990s relative to other time periods. The first thing to realize is that the lower the marginal rate, the less tax-motivated any financial decision should be. Second, be on guard, because marginal tax rates can be (and will be) changed at the whim of Congress. What's wise today regarding tax planning may not be wise next year.

Effective Rate. This is the total amount paid in taxes, divided by the total income earned. In the case of Bob and Laura, they earned $49,600 last year. However, they were allowed exemptions for themselves and their children, as well as itemized deductions for medical expenses, property taxes, state income taxes, and charitable contributions. All of these deductions and exemp-

Top Rate on "Unearned" Income

Year	Top Rate (%)
1936-40	75
1941	77
'42-'43	82
'44-'45	91
'46-'47	83.6
'48-'49	79.4
1950	81.6
1951	87.2
'52-'53	88
'54-'63	87
1964	74
'65-'81	70
'82-'86	50
1987	38.5
1988	33
1989	33
1990	33

tions reduce the total income down to the taxable income. The income taxes are then computed on taxable income.

If we assume that their taxable income was $40,000, then the taxes that they would pay on the $40,000 is $5,700, which represents 11.5 percent of the total income of $49,600. Therefore, we can say that even though they are in the 20 percent tax bracket and will marginally pay 30 percent, they are effectively paying only 11.5 percent of their income in taxes. *The effective rate is the key number*. It is much more important than the tax bracket or marginal rate.

The simple objective in tax planning is to reduce the effective tax rate in order to generate after-tax dollars for any goals that you have.

Living expenses, debt retirement, and investments are three categories of cash-flow requirements that are paid with after-tax dollars in almost every case. Therefore, if the objective is to pay zero taxes, all living expenses, debt retirement, and many investments must be paid with either borrowed funds or not paid at all.

For example, if Bob and Laura decide to pay off their home mortgage of $81,500, that means over time they must generate, after taxes, $81,500 with which to pay that debt. There is no way they can pay the debt with pretax dollars. By the same token, if their objective is to have $30,000 of living expenses this year, then they must generate, after taxes, after giving, and after debt repayment, $30,000. The lower the effective tax rate, the more easily this is accomplished. However, that rate can never go to zero, as I previously explained. The question is, How can you reduce your effective tax rate? Remember, *the effective rate is far more important than the tax bracket or marginal rate*.

TAX PLANNING STRATEGIES

The most popular time for tax planning by taxpayers is December, with the second most popular month being April. However, both months are too late to do any serious tax planning. Once December 31 has passed, nothing can be done, other than an IRA or pension plan investment, to reduce taxes for the previous year. Most people know this and become rather panicky in the month of December, wondering how they are going to reduce their taxes. My general rule for tax planning is:

The shorter the perspective on tax planning, the higher the risk that must be taken and/or the fewer the options that are available.

I believe that most income-tax planning should be done at least one year in advance with monitoring and the necessary adjustments made in the plan at least quarterly during the year. This means that the tax planning you do on December 31 would not be for the current year, but for the next year, so that you are always one year ahead. Tax planning is much like a funnel—at the beginning of the year, the options are many, but as you go through the year, the funnel narrows and the options become fewer. As a stream of liquid passing through the funnel rushes more rapidly near the nozzle, so the emotional intensity increases as the year goes by. The end of the year, with so few options available and so much emotion being generated, is the time when many poor tax planning decisions are made.

All tax planning falls into four general tax planning strategies: timing, shifting, investing, and use of the tax law. You don't need to be an expert to understand these four general strategies, you merely need to ask yourself four questions:

1. *Timing.* Can I reduce my taxes by changing the year I am to receive income or to pay deductible expenses?
2. *Shifting:* Can I reduce my taxes by shifting my income to someone in my family who is in a lower tax bracket?
3. *Investing.* Can I reduce my taxes through the use of investments?
4. *Use of Tax Law.* Can I reduce my taxes through the wise use of any additional tax law provisions that I am not now using?

Timing Strategies

Timing strategies involve the timing of the recognition of income and the deduction of expenses. The general rule is that you should always push income into a future year and pull expenses into the current year. Why? Because, even if it does not change the tax bracket one way or the other, the utilization of a timing strategy does delay the payment of taxes. For example, if a taxpayer is in the 15 percent bracket and has the opportunity to delay $1,000 of income, it will reduce the current taxes by $150; but because that income went into the next year, it increases the taxes paid next year by $150.

That may not seem to make any difference; however, the taxpayer, not the government, has had the use of $150 for one year and the time to earn interest on that $150. Previously, we saw how a little bit over a long period can add up to a great deal through the magic of compounding.

Pulling deductions into the current year has the same effect. For example, if a taxpayer is in the 15 percent tax bracket and pulls $1,000 of deductions from next year into this year, the tax liability goes down $150 for the current year and up $150 for the next year. As above, this strategy enables the taxpayer to control the $150 for a longer time.

The general rule is that you should always push income into a future year and pull expenses into the current year.

In considering this strategy, the doctrine in tax law called the doctrine of constructive receipt must be understood. The doctrine of constructive receipt simply says that if you earn the income and have a right to receive it, you cannot postpone the taxes incurred on that amount by merely choosing not to receive it.

For example, a person offering professional services receives checks near the end of the year, but in an effort to avoid taxable income, he merely sticks them in a bottom drawer and does not deposit them until after December 31. This violates the doctrine of constructive receipt. He is attempting to use a timing strategy in reducing his income, but as a matter of fact, it is tax evasion, not tax avoidance.

There are many legal ways to defer income, such as postponing the work that would generate the income so that the payment received for it is not due until the following year. Also, money invested in a savings type of account, such as a money market fund, is taxed, as the interest is earned on a daily basis. Instead of leaving the money in such an account, invest it in a Treasury Bill that has a maturity date beyond the end of the year. Then the income generated by that investment is taxed in the subsequent year rather than the current year.

A self-employed person can choose to pay bonuses after the end of the calendar year, thereby postponing the tax on that income until the next year. There are other ways to defer income, but my objective here is to challenge your thinking and your own creativity rather than to provide a tax manual.

Some of the obvious ways to pull deductions into the current year are to pay for all expenses incurred, but not yet paid, prior to the end of the year—for example, interest on debt that has been incurred, medical expenses that have been incurred but not yet paid, legal fees, state income taxes, and so on. You cannot, according to the law, prepay interest and medical expenses, but you can bring the payments up to date, thereby deducting them in the current year as opposed to the subsequent year. You will need to be alert for these deductions as delayed billing in December is increasingly common by professionals.

My recommendation is that you review last year's tax return and for each item of income ask yourself, Could it have been deferred into the subsequent year? And for each deduction you took ask, In this area, could I have pulled more deductions from the subsequent year? Because of their nature, timing strategies are about the only strategies that work near the end of the year. Almost all of the other strategies must be implemented earlier in the year.

Shifting Strategies

Understanding tax brackets is essential for understanding shifting strategies. The shifting strategies ask the question, Can I shift what would be taxable income to me to a taxpaying entity in a lower tax bracket? For example, can I shift income from my wife and me, who are in a high tax bracket, to our children, who are in a very low tax bracket, and perhaps pay no taxes at all? The assumption in using this type of strategy is that I can shift the income and either still retain control of that income or use it for an item that I would have paid for anyway.

Probably the classic example of shifting income is in the area of providing for the college education of children. Many times parents will have the opportunity to give their children over the age of thirteen income-producing assets so that the child can pay the income taxes earned on that income rather than the parent and use the income left over after paying taxes to pay for a college education. (Income earned from income-producing assets by children under the age of fourteen is taxed as if it were income earned by the parents.)

For example, if the college education costs are $5,000 per year and the parents are paying that cost, they must earn the $5,000 plus the taxes on that $5,000 in order to have $5,000 left over to pay for the college education. If their tax bracket is 30 percent, then they must earn approximately $7,143 to have $5,000 left over with which to pay education costs. If, on the other hand, the child is in the 15 percent tax bracket, he or she can earn $5,882, pay the taxes, and still have $5,000 left over. The parents, then, have paid for the college education for that year with substantially fewer dollars than had they paid the taxes on their earnings and then funded the college education with after-tax earnings.

The shifting strategy typically works best within a family. The reason this strategy works best within families is that the ultimate objective is not to give away money, but to reduce taxes on income that is earned. You could, for example, give me $10,000 of income-producing assets (which, incidentally, I would gladly accept). However, you are out-of-pocket for the total gift, and even though your income taxes went down, this did not make good economic sense.

Gifting. The shifting strategy involves making a gift to another family member of income-producing assets such as cash, real estate, stocks, bonds, closely held stock and notes, or mortgages receivable. Frequently these items are given in a trust form. The parents and an independent person act as trustee for the child's benefit. The only problem is that a gift literally must be made and the property legally transferred to the other person or trust. It cannot be loaned to them, nor transferred under any type of facade. A gift must actually be made, and if the gift is large enough, a gift tax may have to be paid.

Investments

The purpose of every investment you make is to produce more value or more income over time. Income from investments is taxed in various ways and can, therefore, have a great impact on total taxes paid. Income investments are taxed in four ways.

Tax-exempt. The income from some investments, such as municipal bonds, is tax-exempt by law, and as a result, this income is substantially lower than the fully taxable income earned on similar types of investments.

Tax-deferred. Some investments require that no tax be paid on the income earned until some time in the future. Almost any pension plan falls into this category, whether it is an employer-only contribution or one of your own pension plans such as an IRA, a Keogh plan, S.E.P., or a qualified retirement plan. In addition, tax-deferred annuities sold by brokerage houses and insurance companies allow you to accumulate on a tax-deferred basis.

The value of a tax-deferred investment is that compounding works for you not only on your portion of the income earned on the investment but also on the portion that would have gone to pay taxes, had they not been deferred. Additionally, when it is time to pay taxes on the investment income that has been generated, presumably the investor is retired and in a lower tax bracket, and therefore, in real dollar terms, pays less in income taxes.

Tax-favored. Tax-favored investments are investments having special income tax allowances and provisions, again merely as a matter of law and not because of the nature of the investment. For example, most oil and gas tax investments enjoy a favored status due to the depletion allowance.

Fully taxable. The fourth type of investment is one that is fully taxable and includes almost all interest-bearing types of investments other than those described above.

The principle still needs to be remembered that any time there is a favorable tax consequence to an investment, there is a corresponding cost somewhere. For example, in the tax-exempt investments, the cost is that the yield is not as high as in fully taxable investments. In the case of tax-deferred investments, the cost is the nonliquidity of the investment owing to the penalties associated with withdrawing the monies. In the area of tax-favored investments, the cost is typically in the higher risk associated with those investments.

To give you an idea of the consequences of the taxability of income and what that means in terms of your ability to accumulate, the following chart assumes a $1,000 investment per year. The tax-free investment return is 5 percent; the tax-deferred investment return is 8 percent; the fully-taxable return, also at 8 percent, is assumed at a 25 percent marginal tax rate.

Difference Between "Tax-Free" and "Tax-Defferred"

	5% Tax-free	8% Yield Tax-deferred	8% Yield 25% Tax Bracket
Year 1	$ 1,050	$ 1,080	$ 1,060
Year 5	5,525	5,867	5,637
Year 10	12,578	14,487	13,181
Year 15	21,579	27,152	23,276
Year 20	33,067	45,762	36,786
Year 25	47,727	73,106	54,864
Year 30	66,439	113,283	79,058
Year 35	90,320	172,317	111,435
Year 40	127,800	295,056	154,762

	5% Tax-free	8% Yield Tax-deferred	8% Yield 25% Tax Bracket
Years the fund will last if it continues to earn interest but a withdrawal of $29,500 per year is made	5.0	22.0	6.5

In reviewing the chart, it is easy to see that the tax bracket you are in has a major bearing on the relative attractiveness of the investment. At the end of forty years in the tax-deferred investment, you could begin drawing an amount at 10 percent per year and would have both a return of principal and income in terms of the taxable consequence of that withdrawal. If we assume the withdrawal is 10 percent per year and that all of the withdrawal is interest and fully taxable and the remaining principal continues to earn 8 percent, the tax-deferred fund is still not depleted until twenty-two years in the future. Compare this to withdrawing the same $29,500 per year from the other funds. The tax-free fund is fully depleted after five years and the fully taxable fund in six-and-a-half years.

As you anticipate the end of your accumulation, the tax-free nature of certain income may appear desirable. However, the illustration shows the value of compounding on a tax-deferred basis as compared to any other alternative. Tax-free investments do not yield enough to offset the compounding impact on a tax-deferred basis, nor do they offset the compounding associated with fully taxable amounts for the taxpayer in the 25 percent bracket in this illustration.

The primary point is that there are different types of tax-favored investments. When making an investment decision, the decision, first of all, is an investment decision and, second, a tax decision. However, the taxes can make one more favorable than another.

Use of Tax-Law Provisions

The last strategy to use in tax planning is to review all the tax-law provisions that allow for deductions, deferrals, credits, and the like to make sure you are using all that are applicable to your situation. These provisions are somewhat technical and fill pages of the Internal Revenue Code, so I will explain only the major categories, and then in each category, list some of the tax law provisions that might be applicable. Review these and seek advice from a professional if you think they are applicable.

Adjustments to Income. Adjustments to income are just exactly that—certain expenditures that adjust the income reported on the tax form in order to compute what is called "adjusted gross income." Adjusted gross income is an important number because some deductions on the tax return relate to that number. The most common adjustments allowable to income are IRA payments, Keogh payments, and S.E.P. payments of self-employed individuals.

Itemized Deductions. Some itemized deductions that are allowable are medical and dental expenses; state and local taxes, including property taxes, income taxes, and all personal property taxes; certain interest paid (mainly interest paid on home mortgages and on investment property); charitable contributions of either cash or property; moving expenses; and investment related expenses. Some of these items are only deductible if they exceed a percentage of your adjusted gross income for the year.

I am often asked whether contributions of time are deductible, and the answer is no. If you do not receive an income for the time spent, you have, in effect, already received a deduction by not having the income to report as taxable income.

The most commonly overlooked itemized deductions are:

- Expenses paid as a volunteer for charitable organizations
- Points paid on a purchase of a personal residence
- Personal property taxes

Tax Credits. In addition to deductions and adjustments to income, tax law provides for tax credits that reduce taxes dollar-for-dollar (whereas adjustments and deductions are not dollar-for-dollar).

The principal tax credits include the foreign tax credits, if you pay taxes in a foreign country, child and dependent care credit for expenses paid by a working couple, and certain limited investment tax credits for energy, property, and rehabilitation expenditures.

Special Provisions. In addition, the IRS has special provisions for certain situations such as the deferral of the tax on the gain from the sale of a principal residence, exemptions for each dependent, and for many, many other situations and items.

Using the tax-law provisions typically requires expert counsel, but you should also personally review the tax-return package sent to you by the government very thoroughly. Because preparation of the tax return is distasteful to most of us, we often fail to pay close enough attention to all of the provisions that will help us reduce our taxes.

Special Opportunity. Ours is one of the few countries in the world that allows charitable deductions for income-tax purposes. One of the principal advantages that our government allows in this area is the deduction of the full fair-market value of a gift of property. For example, if you purchased a stock for $10,000 and it has appreciated in value to $20,000, and if you sold that stock and paid the tax on it of, say, $2,800, you would have $17,200 left to give to a charitable organization. The $17,200 contribution would further reduce your taxes by (for illustration purposes) 28 percent or $4,816, so that the net cost of making the charitable contribution would be the $20,000 property less the $4,816 tax savings or $15,184.

If, on the other hand, the stock had been contributed directly to the charitable organization, there would have been a $20,000 contribution allowed, with a tax savings of $5,600, for a net cost of $14,400. The charity, in turn, could sell the property for $20,000 and have $20,000 rather than $17,200, and it would have cost the taxpayer $784 less ($5,600–$4,816) to give a charity $2,800 more ($20,000–$17,200). Obviously, this is a "win-win" situation. The following chart illustrates this opportunity for taxpayers in various tax brackets.

Give Cash

	15% Tax Bracket	28% Tax Bracket	33% Tax Bracket
Sales Price	$20,000	$20,000	$20,000
Tax on Gain	(1,500)	(2,800)	(3,300)
Given to Charities	18,500	17,200	16,700
Tax Savings	$ 2,775	$ 4,816	% 5,511
Cost to Giver:			
Stock Value	$20,000	$20,000	$20,000

Less Tax Savings	(2,775)	(4,816)	(5,511)
Actual Cost	$17,225	$15,184	$14,489

GIVE PROPERTY

Given to Charity	$20,000	$20,000	$20,000
Tax Savings	(3,000)	(5,600)	(6,600)
Actual Cost	$17,000	$14,400	$13,400
Difference	$ 225	$ 784	$ 1,089

One important caveat in contributing appreciated property is that the appreciation amount, while not subject to regular tax, is subject to the Alternative Minimum Tax, if you fall into that category. If you suspect you may be in Alternative Minimum Tax (or are contributing a substantially appreciated asset) see a tax professional for help.

Action to Be Taken

As a taxpayer you need to take three steps. First, determine the projected tax liability for the following year as early in the year as possible; second, plan to reduce that liability through the many items discussed here; and third, set the withholding amount and the tax-estimate amount at the projected liability amount.

No taxpayer has to pay more estimated tax or withholding greater than his last year's liability or 90 percent of his current year's liability, whichever one is less. Again, as I said earlier, to receive a tax refund is a sign of poor planning. I recommend that you determine your projected tax liability simply by taking last year's tax return and projecting to the best of your knowledge what the numbers will be this year, using the Income Tax Analysis worksheet that follows.

Your Income Tax Analysis

	Last Year	Estimated This Year
INCOME		
Salary	_____	_____
Interest & Dividends	_____	_____

	Last Year	Estimated This Year
INCOME		
New Business Income (Schedule C)	_____	_____
State Tax Refund	_____	_____
Schedule D Income	_____	_____
Schedule E Income	_____	_____
Other	_____	_____
GROSS INCOME	_____	_____
LESS ADJUSTMENTS TO INCOME:		
IRA/Keogh	_____	_____
Other	_____	_____
Adjusted Gross Income (A.G.I.)	_____	_____
LESS ITEMIZED DEDUCTIONS:		
Medical Expenses over 7.5% of A.G.I.	_____	_____
Taxes	_____	_____
Interest	_____	_____
Contributions	_____	_____
Miscellaneous over 2% of A.G.I.	_____	_____
Moving Expenses	_____	_____
Total Deductions	_____	_____
LESS EXEMPTIONS	_____	_____
TAXABLE INCOME	_____	_____
FEDERAL INCOME TAX	_____	_____
PLUS OTHER TAXES:		
Self-employment Tax	_____	_____
Other	_____	_____
LESS CREDITS	_____	_____
TOTAL FEDERAL TAX	_____	_____
TOTAL STATE TAX	_____	_____
TOTAL TAX	_____	_____

MARGINAL TAX RATE   _____   _____

EXCESSIVE TAX RATE   _____   _____

After completing this worksheet, determine the withholding amounts paid to date for the year, compared to what will be paid if the withholdings stay at the same level. If needed, you can adjust the withholding to the newly determined amount. In 1988 over 72 million taxpayers got an average refund of $819. In effect, what they had done was make an $819 interest-free loan to the government for one year.

In Bob and Laura's case, they determined that by changing their W-4 to reduce withholdings to the rate that coincides with what they would actually receive, they could generate an additional $2,500 of cash flow this year. Additionally, they need to make a decision about whether or not to do an IRA for both of them. Laura has $2,000 of self-employment income, which could be used to fund an IRA, and of course Bob could fund one also. Because they do not have the excess cash flow to do so, they would have to decide whether that money should come out of their savings account. The chances are that they should, but we will discuss that option for them later.

Concluding Comments on Tax Planning

Tax planning must be integrated with all other types of planning. However, tax planning should not be the tail that wags the dog; it should rather remain the tail. Investment planning requires, first of all, that you make a good investment and then consider the tax consequences, rather than make the investment for tax consequences. That goes for charitable contributions, estate planning, and any other type of financial decision.

Tax planning is very important, but it is not a panacea for cash flow problems. Every decision that causes a reduction in taxes has a corresponding cost associated with it. Therefore, reducing taxes may increase cash flow in the short term, but there is a cost associated with it, and that must be considered. Just remember, there is no free lunch, especially in the cafeteria of tax reductions.

Tax planning can and will change as Congress changes tax laws, as the IRS decides how to administer the law, and as the courts interpret the law. The principles contained in this chapter almost certainly *won't* change as long as we have a graduated income-tax system, but the specific application may vary as laws are changed.

INVESTMENT PLANNING

People tend to think that since I am a Christian financial planner I am against acquiring material possessions or accumulations of cash. Once when Judy and I were with a couple, the woman showed us a very large diamond she was wearing, and then quickly explained that the diamond was an "investment." I smiled and wondered to myself how high the price of diamonds would have to go before that diamond would be sold. I doubt that diamond would be taken off the woman's finger for any price.

An investment is something that is purchased with the intent to resell at a higher price. Therefore, diamonds, expensive cars, vacation homes, and antiques never qualify as investments. They are purchases that may go up in value and consequently prove to be a wise purchase, but they are not investments. Many people delude themselves into calling a purchase an investment in order to justify buying it, but it is never an investment unless it was purchased to preserve or increase its value, and ultimately, to resell it at a higher price than what was paid for it, or for it to provide some amount of economic return or yield.

It is critical that you understand the difference between an investment and a purchase, because different criteria are used to evaluate each one. In this section, we will only be dealing with investments—things purchased solely to generate a yield to the investor, or to grow in value, or to do both. If they are not accomplishing the intended objective, then they should be sold immediately.

The Most Common Investment Mistakes

I am in the enviable position of representing clients who, for the most part, have fairly significant sums of discretionary dollars each year to invest. As such, they are approached regularly with "good deals," and our firm is constantly barraged with good deals to present to our clients.

Obviously, not all of these deals are good deals. But on the front end, they always seem to be. Good deals only become bad deals over time, and I have learned something: *There will be as good a deal tomorrow as there is today*. Therefore, I never have to respond to the "good deal" that is presented to me today regardless of how good it is, because my experience has shown that I will have another one tomorrow, and another one the next day, and another one the next day, and another one the next day.

I call this dilemma the "binary trap." The binary trap centers on the question, Should I do this or not? It only gives me two alternatives—yes or no—and if the deal is a good deal I most certainly should say yes to it. However, the binary trap begs the real question, What is the best use of these discretionary funds? When I ask the question that way, I immediately open up many more alternatives to investing than just the one presented.

Unless there is a long-term investment strategy in place, you will always be subject to falling into the binary trap. The investment for any investor depends upon one's personal long-term goals and the strategy to accomplish those goals. Then any investment that comes along is selected as a means to meet the goals in light of the strategy, as opposed to assuming that every good investment is something that everyone should participate in.

Rather than looking at specific investments (a major topic that needs to be covered in a separate book), I feel it is more important for you to develop and to understand your strategy. Then individual investments, as they come along, can be evaluated in light of your strategy rather than the reverse—setting your strategy on the basis of the investments you have made.

From an investment standpoint, we have basically two time periods of life. The time period when we are accumulating to meet long-term goals I simply call the accumulation phase. In this phase of life we are accumulating not only material possessions but also investments for the purpose of accomplishing our long-term goals of financial independence or starting our own business.

Once the long-term goals have been met and we have accumulated enough by that definition, we enter the second phase of investing—the preservation phase. In the preservation phase we want to preserve the assets we have accumulated in light of the various risks that we face, such as inflation, deflation, monetary collapse, and interest rates going up and down.

The diagram on page 184 illustrates these two time periods of an investor's life. Basically, from age twenty to approximately age forty, we are accumulating material possessions, paying off debt, and raising our families. The major accumulation begins to take place between the ages of forty and fifty, and at some point during this time period we may cross the line of having accumulated enough to meet our long-term goals. However, almost no one stops accumulating at this point for one very good reason—the uncertainty of

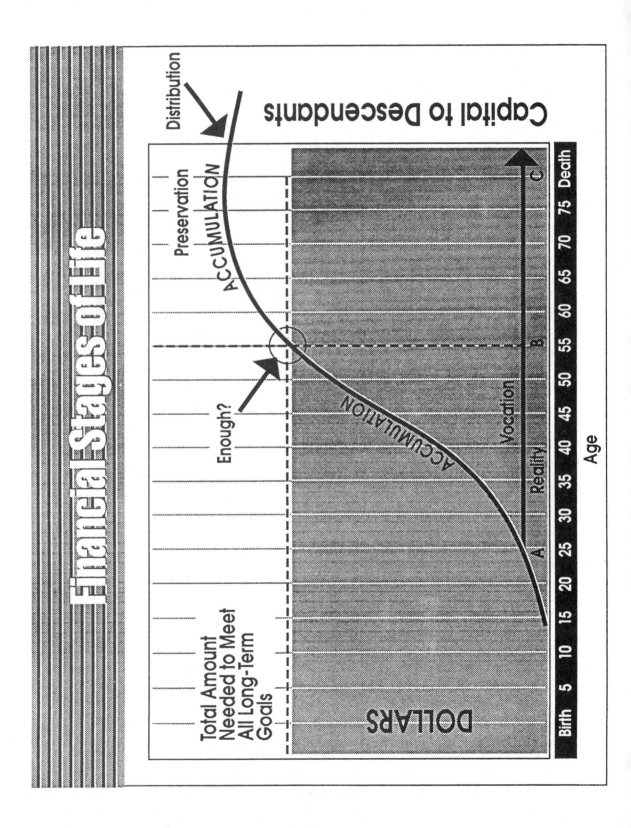

Financial Stages of Life

Distribution

Capital to Descendants

Preservation

ACCUMULATION

Enough?

Total Amount
Needed to Meet
All Long-Term
Goals

ACCUMULATION

DOLLARS

Vocation

Reality

Birth 5 10 15 20 25 30 35 40 45 50 55 60 65 70 75 Death

A B C

Age

our economic environment. Sometime around the age of sixty, we shift to a preservation mode where we are attempting to preserve our assets in light of the risks.

Then at some point between sixty and eighty, we enter the distribution phase. The distribution phase of investment planning can either be immediate, in the event of death, or planned to take place over a long term. We will discuss the distribution phase of life next week.

Obviously, the graph will be different for different people. Some of us achieve our long-term goals very clearly; others of us never achieve our long-term goals. The point is to understand where you are and what that means for your investment strategy. You need to know if you are in an accumulation strategy or a preservation strategy because the investment techniques and the type of investments to be considered are different for each of the strategies.

It is also important to know what level of accumulation (represented by the line on the graph) is needed to meet the long-term goals. That number and that line define how much is enough. When you go beyond that line, you have to answer the question, Why am I continuing to accumulate?

The two key questions to ask yourself when considering investing and an investment strategy are: (1) Why am I investing? (What long-term goal will this investment help to meet?) and (2) What is my purpose—accumulation or preservation?

ACCUMULATION STRATEGY

The basic philosophy that I have been attempting to communicate throughout this book is that a little bit over a long time period will allow you to accomplish your long-term goals. The alternative is to get rich quick and live with the high risk of losing it all. Most people invest by responding rather than by planning. I hope by this point you are convinced that planning your investments, rather than responding to the alternatives presented to you, is a far more secure path to achieving your long-term financial goals.

First of all, the accumulation strategy revolves around having a cash-flow margin and then making a decision regarding the use of this margin. You say, "The best use of this margin is _____." The "best" will depend on four things: your personal goals, the commitments you already have, your personal priorities, and all the other alternatives for spending this margin.

I have a recommendation for the sequential use of your cash-flow margin, and I call it the Sequential Investment Strategy. With this investment strat-

SEQUENTIAL INVESTMENT STRATEGY

Rules to keep in mind:

- *A positive cash flow is required.*
- *Don't even think of investing unless you have taken Steps 1 & 2.*

1

Eliminate all high-interest/short term debt.

(1) Credit Cards
(2) Automobiles
(3) Small Debt

2

Keep one month's living expenses in an interest bearing checking acct.

*Living Expenses determined from your monthly budget.

3

Keep 3–6 Months' living expenses in a Money Market Fund (MMF) or Savings Acct.

*Reserves to protect in case of disability, accidents, or any emergency.

4

Put savings for major purchases in a MMF, CD, or Treasury (potentially a Mutual Fund).

(1) Automobiles
(2) Furniture
(3) Down payment towards house.

5

Invest to meet long term goals in:

- MMF/CD's/Treasuries
- Mutual Funds
- Real Estate
- Bonds
- Equities

(1) Retirement
(2) College for Children
(3) Financial Freedom
(4) Lake House
(5) Travel

6

Speculate:

- Hard Assets
- Venture Capital

(1) Develop your own business.
(2) Extra Gifting:
  —Church
  —Children

egy, you use the first dollar of cash-flow margin to accomplish Step 1, and all additional dollars of margin to accomplish each step in sequence. The strategy is as follows:

Step 1: Eliminate all credit card and consumer debt. This, as explained earlier, provides an immediate "investment return" of 12 percent to 21 percent. Not having to pay that interest cost each year is, in effect, the same as achieving the same rate of return on any monies invested by you. Therefore, it is the surest and highest form of investment return you can make.

Step 2: Set aside one month's living expenses in the checking account. This is in addition to the current month's living expenses that are in the checking account, so at the beginning of any one month there would be two month's living expenses already deposited in the checking account. This "investment" is for flexibility.

Step 3: Invest between two and six month's living expenses in an interest-bearing money market fund account. This becomes the emergency fund and, in effect, your own bank. As you need money to make a major purchase or have an unexpected major expense or see an opportunity to save through purchasing now instead of later, you can borrow from yourself out of this account rather than from a lending institution. Once the money has been borrowed, it should, of course, be replaced. Steps 2 and 3 provide you with flexibility so that you will have financial resources in cases of emergency.

Step 4: Save in an interest-bearing account for major purchases. This is the planned purchase of major items such as automobiles, furniture, and even the down payment on a home.

Steps 1 through 4 should be done in sequence rather than all at once. In other words, you do not go to Step 3 until you have accomplished Step 2. By doing so, you eliminate the need to make a decision whenever an investment alternative comes to you. If you have not already accomplished Steps 1 through 4, you let the option go by.

Step 5: Invest to meet long-term goals. The long-term goals of financial independence, college education, giving, owning your own business, paying off debt, and major lifestyle changes, as depicted in your financial planning diagram, are now funded through various investment alternatives. These investment alternatives, however, will have one characteristic—they will be almost risk free because you are still accumulating to meet your long-term goals and therefore have no dollars left with which to speculate.

Step 6: Use investment dollars to speculate in higher risk investments. At this point, by definition, every short-term and long-term goal has already been met. I have seen very few people ever reach this step of investing, and coincidentally, those who have don't like to speculate because they don't want to risk the loss. They prefer to adopt what I have called the "preservation investment strategy."

Let me repeat that *the sequential investment strategy is totally dependent upon having a positive cash-flow margin*. As you have a positive cash flow, the first-priority use of that cash is Step 1, and so forth, in sequence. This sequence obviously represents my opinion about what the priorities should be; your priorities may be different. For example, Step 4 may be a higher priority for you than my Step 3, and that is perfectly acceptable. The important point is to prayerfully set your priorities and to have a strategy for meeting them.

You may even decide to do your investing concurrently rather than sequentially. I believe Steps 1 and 2 must be met first, but then Steps 3, 4, and 5 could be met concurrently with the cash-flow margin for the year allocated in the following way:

To Step 3	40%	30%	?%
To Step 4	40%	Or 60%	Or ?%
To Step 5	20%	10%	?%
Total	100%	100%	100%

Do not forget your strategy and become involved in premature investing and speculating.

Tools and Techniques

In addition to understanding specific investment products, such as stocks, bonds, treasury bills, gold, silver, land, mutual funds, and apartments, you need to know the tools and techniques for investing these specific products. For example, an IRA is a tool allowed by the government and basically the same type of tool as any pension plan. Dollar-cost averaging, which is a strategy of committing a fixed amount of money per month to a particular investment resulting in a low per-unit cost, is a technique of investing. Market timing is a technique of buying and selling stocks or mutual funds according to a mathematical formula resulting over time, one hopes, in selling near the top of the market and buying near the bottom of the market.

Each of these tools and/or techniques uses one of the specific investment products to accomplish its objective. The techniques require a great deal of experience and expertise to be effective and should be utilized by the investor only with assistance by an expert. The tools, such as an IRA, require merely that the investor know whether the tool fits his or her situation and then how to implement the tool through the use of one of the products.

The tools and techniques can be used either during the accumulation or the preservation phase of investing.

Specific Investments

For those who are still accumulating, I recommend three primary types of investments:

1. Money Market Instruments. These investment products are liquid and yielding with very little risk of loss of principal except in an inflationary time. Specifically, these investments would include certificates of deposit, treasury bills, savings accounts, and money-market funds.

The advantage of a money-market-fund type of investment or any other short-term, interest-bearing investment is that you have professional money managers managing your investment in order to achieve the highest return at the lowest risk while maintaining total liquidity of the investment. Therefore, you don't have to guess about whether interest rates are going up or down, and you always have the opportunity to move the money out of the money-market fund if a better investment comes along.

2. Growth Mutual Funds. A mutual fund is, in effect, a pooled fund of money from many investors that is entrusted to a professional money manager. There are almost as many types of mutual funds as there are investment objectives. The three main types are: long-term growth funds that invest primarily in the stock market, income funds that invest basically in high-yielding types of investments, and a combination of income and growth funds that attempt to achieve both objectives.

The advantage of using mutual funds for accumulation is that you achieve professional management, diversification in your investments, total liquidity of the funds, and you can choose a fund that fits your specific goals, such as growth or income.

3. Real Estate Investments. This type of accumulation investment is comprised of either personally owned rental-type real estate or public real estate partnerships. Personally owned real estate can typically take a great deal of experience and time with a fairly high risk, especially for the novice. On the other hand, you can invest in public real estate partnerships for as little as $1,000 to $5,000 and still accomplish the goals of growth through real estate without having a substantial sum of money or expertise. Once investors move into private placement real estate investments, my recommendation is that they always use an expert counselor to choose the specific investment.

Preservation Investment Strategy

The perfect investment is one that is totally liquid, with no risk, yielding a high percentage of return, and growing at a rate greater than the inflation rate. I have yet to see the perfect investment because there are always trade-offs. An investment that is liquid typically does not grow much in value—for example, a savings account. On the other hand, one that is growing in value, such as real estate, probably bears some risk, may not have a yield associated with it, and certainly is not liquid.

A good investment strategy for the entire investment portfolio accomplishes four specifically quantified universal investment objectives: (1) maximize liquidity, (2) maximize growth, (3) maximize yield, and (4) minimize risk. Of these four objectives, investors will have different priorities that are dependent upon a variety of things.

Age. A younger person needs less liquidity, takes more risk, needs more growth, and can accept less yield.

Temperament. Some people can stand no risk and want all of their money invested in certificates of deposit. Others have the philosophy, "Let's roll the dice."

Tax situation. Those in the higher tax brackets are more typically concerned with growth than they are yield because the tax on the growth is deferred, whereas yield is typically taxed in the current higher-income tax brackets.

Other financial commitments. A debt may need to be repaid in the near future or lifestyle commitments for the near future may require more liquidity than at other times.

Certainty of future cash flow. Some people have a certainty of future cash flow through pension plans, other retirement plans, or Social Security, and the yield factor is less important for them than the growth factor. Others may have no retirement income, and therefore the yield factor is far more important to them.

The point is that each of these four universal investment objectives can be quantified, dependent upon your age, temperament, tax situation, personal philosophy, perception, and goals. Then an investment portfolio can be designed that is measurable in terms of its ability to accomplish the objectives that have been set.

TYPES OF RISK

Once the investment portfolio has been designed and its ability to meet the universal investment objectives measured, an evaluation of the "risk" in the portfolio needs to be done. It used to be simple to define risk as merely the loss of principal. Money stored or hidden stood the risk of thieves and erosion, whereas money invested in a bank stood the risk of bank failures. However, for the most part, the risk was well known and could be planned for. Once an investment portfolio becomes sizeable and once we introduce a worldwide and a very uncertain economic situation, the risks become far more complex and more difficult to plan for. For example:

Business risk. Some investments such as a real estate project or a specific stock are dependent upon the successful running of a business in order for the principal to remain intact.

Financial risk. Some investments will retain their relative value in times of monetary collapse or total economic or political upheaval whereas others won't. For example, during a monetary collapse, real estate and gold may retain their relative value whereas cash probably will not. Many investments, therefore, bear some financial risk.

Market risks. No one has total control of the market; rather we are subject to whatever market we happen to be investing in, whether it is the real estate market or the stock market or the bond market. Any investment that is a part of a larger market bears a risk that is basically uncontrollable by any one individual.

Interest-rate risk. Many investments will provide a current interest rate, but if that interest rate is fixed and interest rates for similar types of investments go up, you have borne an interest-rate risk. As an investment strategy, it used to be safe when interest rates were less volatile to invest in long-term, nontaxable municipal bonds yielding 3 percent, 4 percent, 5 percent, or 6 percent. The interest rate was known, and if you then locked that interest rate in for a long time period, you were relatively safe.

Purchasing power risk. Investments in cash-type investments, such as certificates of deposit, money market funds, savings accounts, treasury bills, among other instruments, experience a loss in purchasing power during times of inflation, whereas in times of deflation, they experience an increase in purchasing power.

Tax risk. Many investments, such as tax shelters, have a risk of future assessments associated with them because the IRS may change the law or their interpretation of the law. An investment in cash probably bears no tax risk, whereas an investment in an opal mine in Brazil, yielding a five to one tax write-off, might bear a substantial tax risk.

Legal risks. Certain investments may have a risk of lawsuits associated with them. For example, if you are investing in rental real estate, you certainly bear the risk of a lawsuit if someone is injured on your property.

There are three ways to reduce the risk taken in any one investment or on the whole investment portfolio. First of all, become personally knowledgeable about investments and the risk you are taking before entering into an investment. Second, use experts since no one can be an expert in everything. (However, the burden of taking the risk is always on the investor rather than on the advisor.)

Third, do not attempt to guess the future, but rather diversify your investments so that some will be worth more over time while others will be worth less over time, depending on changing economic situations. If all investments have been properly diversified, the overall impact is that the investment portfolio has been preserved in total relative value.

Remember this key point because your strategy is a preservation strategy rather than an accumulation strategy. All of the accumulating has already been done. Now you are preserving the assets or investments relative to all of the risks and relative to the goals and objectives that you have. If you knew with certainty the future, you would not diversify; you would put all of your eggs in one basket. The best way to prepare for the future and to preserve the investments that you have accumulated is to diversify, diversify, and diversify again.

There is absolutely no way to avoid all risks, and quite frankly, the number-one objective is not necessarily to avoid all the risks. God owns all of my investments and your investments and is in total control of the situation. If I am counting on having a risk-free investment portfolio to give me peace of mind, I will never accomplish it. The Bible has much to say about investments—more about attitude toward handling investments than about how to make investments.

BIBLICAL PRINCIPLES OF INVESTING

Do not presume upon the future. "Come now, you who say, 'Today or tomorrow we will go to such and such a city, spend a year there, buy and sell, and make a profit'; whereas you do not know what will happen tomorrow. For what is your life? It is even a vapor that appears for a little time and then vanishes away. Instead you ought to say, 'If the Lord wills, we shall live and do this or that'" (James 4:13–15).

Avoid speculation and hasty investment decisions. "A faithful man will abound with blessings,/But he who hastens to be rich will not go unpunished" (Prov. 28:20). "A man with an evil eye hastens after riches,/And does not consider that poverty will come upon him" (Prov. 28:22). "Dishonest money dwindles away,/but he who gathers money little by little makes it grow" (Prov. 13:11 NIV).

Never cosign. "Do not be one of those who shakes hands in a pledge,/One of those who is surety for debts;/If you have nothing with which to pay,/Why should he take away your bed from under you?" (Prov. 22:26–27). "He who is surety for a stranger will suffer,/But he who hates being surety is secure" (Prov. 11:15). "A man devoid of understanding shakes hands in a pledge,/And becomes surety for his friend" (Prov. 17:18).

Evaluate the risk of an investment. "For which of you, intending to build a tower, does not sit down first and count the cost, whether he has enough to finish it" (Luke 14:28). In other words, is the risk that you are taking worth it? Why are you taking the risk? If the risk does happen, can you afford to lose your investment dollar? Will that change anything for you financially?

Avoid investments that cause anxiety. "LORD, my heart is not haughty,/Nor my eyes lofty./Neither do I concern myself with great matters,/Nor with things too profound for me" (Ps. 131:1). "Therefore do not worry, saying, 'What shall we eat?' or 'What shall we drink?' or 'What shall we wear?'" (Matt. 6:31).

Be in unity with your spouse. Throughout Scripture we are admonished to counsel together and to have a unity in the husband/wife relationship. Often God uses our mates to bring us back to reality. Don't be so foolish or proud as not to take advantage of the partner God has given you (1 Peter 3:7–8).

Avoid high-leverage situations. "The rich rules over the poor,/And the borrower is servant to the lender" (Prov. 22:7).

Avoid deceit. "The wicked man does deceptive work,/But he who sows righteousness will have a sure reward" (Prov. 11:18).

Tithe from the current increase rather than the final sale. Many investors believe that it makes good sense to keep the investment dollars and their increases to make additional investments. Usually the rationale is that they will receive greater tax advantages and be able to multiply these resources even more for the Lord. This rationale is unscriptural because God expects a portion of the increase. "Honor the LORD with your possessions,/And with the firstfruits of all your increase;/So your barns will be filled with plenty,/And your vats will overflow with new wine" (Prov. 3:9–10).

To put off giving under the assumption that the investment will earn more and then you will have more to give is a great danger. This assumption implies that God is incapable of using His money today for a greater eternal impact than what I can do by investing.

General Rules in Selection of Investments

We have discussed common investment mistakes, strategies, tools, and techniques, the four investment criteria, risks, diversification, and biblical principles. In many ways all investment planning boils down to some very commonsense general rules.

Always maintain a long-term perspective. The longer the term of perspective, the better the decision is apt to be today.

Remember that you can't be an expert on everything. Be willing to trust others and avoid the pitfall of pride.

High risk to one person is conservative to another. If a person understands the stock market, stock investments may seem conservative. Another may understand nothing about the stock market, and all stock investments appear to be high risks. An oil and gas investment may be conservative to an oil and gas expert; to the uninitiated in this type of investment, it is almost always a high-risk venture.

The personal time required to manage an investment must be considered as a cost. Many investments, such as stock portfolios, rental property, and venture capital, require personal time to ensure that they work out as they are planned. This is a very real cost of the investment, and the benefit, in relation to the cost, must be measured.

Always invest from a strategy. To do otherwise will always put you in the position of being a responder to investment alternatives as they come along. Knowing what your strategy is and the steps to accomplish this strategy will eliminate almost all investment alternatives that are proposed. Hearing about a "good deal" does not necessarily make it a good deal for you.

Keep it simple. My general rule is that if you can't explain it to your spouse, then you don't understand it, and you shouldn't do it. If an investment becomes burdensome and seemingly complex, you are probably in an area of investing that you should not be in.

There is no free lunch. There is a definite risk/reward relationship—the higher the return you expect, the higher the risk you take. With no exception, a high return will exact a high cost.

Diversify, diversify, diversify. Never put all your eggs in one basket. This is the time-tested rule of investing.

The Results of Diversification Chart that follows illustrates how diversification of a total investment portfolio can work to reduce overall risk and increase overall return. Note, however, that not all investments go up in value all the time. It takes a very mature attitude to diversify.

The summary statement of what I have been saying is that very few people should be involved in the high-stakes investment game because almost no one has reached the level of Step 6 of the Sequential Investment Strategy. By following the Sequential Investment Strategy you will, by the time of your need, have accomplished almost all of your long-term goals and objectives.

Investing is not difficult, but it certainly can be confusing if you don't keep your priorities straight.

Results of Diversification

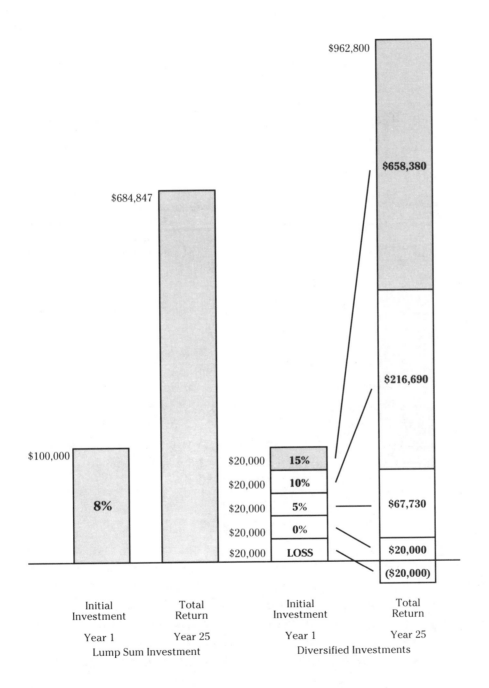

Stewardship After Death

Determining Your Needs for Life Insurance and Estate Planning

---

Session Comments:

> This week's session on life insurance and estate planning is more educational than pro-active. You may want to review this information now, yet plan to use this material for reference when considering future decisions. If you have not considered estate planning or do not currently have a will, I strongly advise that you seek professional counsel.

You may have heard about a family who was gathered in the attorney's office eagerly awaiting the reading of the last will and testament of a recently departed family member. It did not take the attorney long to read the very simple will, which merely stated, "Being of sound mind, I spent it all." I have seen bumper stickers in a similar vein, especially near retirement communities, which say, "We're spending our kids' inheritance."

The assumption underlying both quotations is that you can know exactly when and under what circumstances you are going to die. If that is the case, you could plan to have the last penny spent at the moment of death. Unfortunately, the most frequent comment you hear is that "poor John didn't plan on dying so soon" even though "it is appointed for men to die once, but after this the judgment" (Heb. 9:27). Everyone will die; yet very few plan on "dying so soon."

Another reality is found in 1 Timothy 6:7: "For we brought nothing into this world, and it is certain we can carry nothing out." To paraphrase that verse, "You never see a hearse pulling a U-Haul." John D. Rockefeller's accountant was asked one time, "Can you tell me how much Rockefeller left?" and the accountant said, "Absolutely. Everything."

Our perspective on estate planning is based on these realities: *We will all die, we will take nothing with us, and we will probably die at a time other than we would like.* These realities create many practical planning problems.

PROBLEMS ASSOCIATED WITH DEATH

The most significant problem associated with death is described in Romans 6:23: "For the wages of sin is death, but the gift of God is eternal life in Christ Jesus our Lord." He who dies without having accepted the gift of Jesus Christ as payment for his own sin is eternally separated from God.

Financial problems are nonexistent in eternity. My prayer is that if any of you reading these words has never accepted the free gift of God's Son as payment for your sins, you will do so and make the most important estate planning step you can ever take. A simple prayer lays the foundation for this estate: "Father, I acknowledge my separation from You, and based upon the death of the Lord Jesus Christ as payment for my sins, I accept the free gift of salvation. Thank You for saving me."

Prior to April of 1974, my life's philosophy could have been summed up by another bumper sticker that you may have seen: "He who dies with the most toys wins." Obviously, that is a delusion because the only one who wins when he dies is the one who has the guarantee of eternal life.

The second problem associated with death is really a set of problems relating to your finances. *Unless you plan the distribution of your estate, the government will.* Your spouse, relatives, or friends are not allowed to plan that distribution—only the owner of the assets can plan the distribution through a will. Very rarely does the government have the same objectives for your estate as you do. Additionally, if proper planning has not been done, the final expenses can siphon off up to 70 percent of an estate. These expenses are for probating the will, estate taxes, inheritance taxes, attorney's fees, accountant's fees, and funeral expenses.

Another financial problem that happens frequently because of poor planning is an estate without enough liquidity to meet the final expenses. Therefore, assets must be sold at depressed values just to generate the cash needed to pay these expenses.

Parents with young children rarely plan to die; yet if they do so without proper planning, the state will determine the guardians of those surviving children. Many times, children also have special needs that call for planning if the parents are not going to be around to handle those needs.

Another problem that is associated with death, or as the life insurance industry puts it, "premature death," is that survivors usually experience handling the details of an estate only once. Consequently, there are few experts and fewer yet who can be explicitly trusted to do things exactly as you would have them to. Therefore, there is a problem of making sure that the administration of the estate is handled as you would have it handled.

Being a good steward *after* death requires sound planning in two areas while you are alive: *life insurance* and *estate planning*. In this chapter I will give you some general guidelines in both areas. However, since this is a very complex area and each individual situation is unique, I recommend you seek wise counsel before taking specific implementation steps. This counsel may require input from professionals such as a tax attorney, life insurance agent, bank trust officer, and financial planner. I simply want to get you started in the process.

LIFE INSURANCE PLANNING

Why insurance? The basic purpose of insurance is to transfer the risk that one is not willing to take (or is unable to take) to someone (or a company) willing to take the risk in return for compensation. In the case of life insurance the object is, first, to protect the family income and net worth growth in the event of death of the breadwinner, and second, to provide protection to maintain the estate in order that it might pass on to heirs, allowing the continuation of capital from one generation to the other. (Using our Financial Planning Diagram, life insurance could be depicted by putting an umbrella over the Growth in Net Worth box as illustrated on page 201.) Thus the risk of loss of income or the erosion of the estate through estate taxes is passed to the insurance company. The same idea applies to the protection of houses, automobiles, and other property. Few individuals could afford to replace a house in the event of loss, so they purchase insurance for it.

The Role of Insurance

```
                    ☂

              ┌──────────────┐
              │  Growth in   │
              │  Net Worth   │
              └──────────────┘
                     │
                     ▼
              ┌──────────────┐
   ┌──────────│ Long-Range   │──────────┐
   │     ┌────│ Objectives   │────┐     │
   ▼     ▼    └──────────────┘    ▼     ▼
┌────────────┐   │         │   ┌────────────┐
│ Financial  │   │         │   │ Starting My│
│Independence│   ▼         ▼   │Own Business│
└────────────┘ ┌──────┐ ┌──────┐ └────────────┘
     ┌─────────┐         ┌─────────┐
     │ College │         │ Giving  │
     └─────────┘         └─────────┘
        ┌──────────┐  ┌───────────┐
        │ Pay Off  │  │ Lifestyle │
        │   Debt   │  │  Desires  │
        └──────────┘  └───────────┘
```

The key theme expounded in insurance sales is "protection." While this is certainly the purpose of insurance, emphasizing it also, unfortunately, induces an attitude of fear. Most insurance is purchased on an emotional rather than a factual basis. This attitude then leads to attempts to provide enough insurance to protect against any unknown. For the Christian, this often leads to a shifting of trust from God to insurance and to an imbalance between amounts being provided and amounts one can afford.

The perspective on insurance changes somewhat if the word *provision* is used instead of "protection." God's purpose for the breadwinner is to provide for his family, according to 1 Timothy 5:8: "But if anyone does not provide for his own, and especially for those of his household, he has denied the faith and is worse than an unbeliever."

Under the biblical system, when the father died, the oldest son took the breadwinner's responsibility. If a man had no son, then his brother undertook the care of the family through the laws God had established for widows and orphans.

At the end of every third year you shall bring out the tithe of your produce of that year and store it up within your gates. And the Levite, because he has no portion nor inheritance with you, and the stranger and the fatherless and the widow who are within your gates, may come and eat and be satisfied, that the LORD your God may bless you in all the work of your hand which you do.

—Deuteronomy 14:28–29

Ideally, these caring functions today would be provided by the body of Christ, the church. Unfortunately, they usually are not, so a vital part of family financial planning today is for continued provision through the use of life insurance.

You may say that purchasing insurance shows a lack of trust in God to provide. Rather, this is the sound-mind principle being put to use. If you did not purchase insurance and you are married and have children, it is possible that your spouse would have to go on welfare (becoming dependent on the government). As a result, your family's spiritual and physical needs could go unmet. Insurance, on the other hand, would give your family the opportunity to continue to live in a proper environment.

How much do you need? You can determine how much you need, using the Insurance Needs Analysis Chart (pages 202–204), by first determining the insurance necessary to meet income goals and then adding to it the amount needed for long-term liquidity needs, such as estate taxes and other major expenses at the time of death (in order to facilitate the transfer of your assets from one generation to the next without tax erosion).

Your Insurance Needs Analysis

Income Goals for the Family
    Living expenses[1]   _____
    Taxes   _____
    Giving   _____
TOTAL INCOME NEEDED   _____

                                                          A

Sources of Income[2]
    Social Security   _____

Pension or retirement plans _____

Annuities or trusts _____

Investment income[3] _____

Spouse working _____

Other _____

TOTAL INCOME AVAILABLE ===============
B

Additional Income Needed (per year)[4] _____
A – B = C

Insurance Required to Provide Income[5]
(Additional income needed x 10) _____
C x 10 = D

Additional funds needed for:

Funeral costs _____

Debt repayment _____

Estate tax and settlement expense _____

Education costs _____

Major purchases _____

_____ _____

_____ _____

TOTAL ADDITIONAL FUNDS NEEDED _____
E

INSURANCE NEEDED[6] _____
E + D = F

Assets Available for Sale:

Real estate _____

Stocks, bonds _____

Savings available
(to meet needs listed above)[7] _____

_____ _____

_____ _____

_____ _____

TOTAL FROM SALE OF ASSETS

                                                                                         G

TOTAL INSURANCE NEEDED[8]

$F - G = H$

INSURANCE AVAILABLE NOW

I

ADDITIONAL INSURANCE NEEDED

$H - I = K$

Notes

(1) Use 80 percent of present annual living expense.
(2) Income anticipated on a regular basis.
(3) Income from investments not liquidated.
(4) The total income needed less the total income available $(B - A = C)$.
(5) This assumes the life insurance proceeds could be invested at 10 percent and provide the needed amounts. The investment percentage may be contingent on economic conditions or investment knowledge. The multiplication factor is 1 divided by the percentage return on insurance proceeds. Example: $10\% = 1/.10 = 10; 8\% = 1/.08 = 12.5; 12\% = 1/.12 = 8.33$
(6) Insurance needed is the sum of insurance to provide income (D) plus additional funds needed (E).
(7) Savings available would be only that part of savings that could be applied to meet the needs listed above. It would not include the savings needed to meet family living goals.
(8) Total insurance needed is the insurance needed less the amount available from the sale of assets $(F - G = H)$.

How long do you need it? A key distinction in the Insurance Needs Analysis is the need for current provision and long-term provision. A clear delineation can help you decide between term insurance and a more permanent product.

Typically, when you are young and in the accumulation stage, and having a growing family and a lot of "current" needs (debt, education, and living expenses), you have a large need for insurance but usually limited funds with which to buy the insurance. This usually requires a purchase of term insurance.

Some consumer groups claim that buying term is always the only way to go. However, the idea of buying term and "investing the difference" is based on a short-term perspective. Although it may be sufficient to meet current needs and is much less expensive than whole-life insurance, it does get more expensive over time.

In addition, there are two good reasons to have insurance for a long-term need. First, you may need to have insurance available in your sixties or seventies in order to pay any estate taxes that will be due on a nonliquid estate. You may have a closely held business or some significant nonliquid assets that you want to pass on to your heirs. If you take the approach of buying term, at some point the term insurance will become cost prohibitive and you will no longer have it, thus reducing your options. This points to the second reason to have a long-term insurance plan: flexibility. In your thirties and forties you do not know what your situation will be when you are in your sixties. Having a cornerstone of permanent insurance available at that stage in your life is simply wise planning—looking down the road and counting the cost.

Therefore, the issue of how long you need insurance is difficult to resolve because no one knows what the future holds. But if the need is strictly short-term and will never be any longer than that, then the obvious solution is term insurance. However, if there is an outside chance that estate taxes must be paid or if you want to build in some flexibility for long-term planning, then you should consider some type of permanent insurance for part of your coverage as soon as you can afford it.

What Type of Insurance Product Do You Need?

Although insurance comes in hundreds of "wrappers," there are basically four different types of insurance policies. These are term (such as ART and level-premium five- and ten-year products), traditional whole life, the hybrid product (a combination of whole life and term), and universal life.

Annual renewable term. This product provides the maximum insurance coverage for the lowest initial premiums, with premiums increasing annually. The premium costs at older ages (age sixty to life expectancy) are prohibitive and make it difficult to maintain this type of policy until death. This product does not allow any flexibility in premium payments to meet changing circumstances. The obvious advantage of this type of coverage is the low initial cost, while the not-so-obvious disadvantage is the high cost during the later years.

In general, young families will provide the majority of their insurance needs with term insurance.

Traditional whole life insurance. This product is more expensive initially than a term policy because of the level premiums and cash-value buildup the policy calls for. In a sense, the insurance owner overpays in the early years in order to underpay (or not pay) in later years. It is this aspect of a whole life policy that gives rise to the accumulation of cash value in the policy. This "forced savings" aspect of a whole life policy has been a controversial subject for many years. While many people indicate they do not need to do this, my experience has shown that most people do a poor job of saving for the future, so this aspect of a whole life policy is usually helpful. Even though the policy contract may require premiums to be paid for a certain length of time (that is, one's lifetime), the policy may be paid up much sooner with the use of dividends. The primary disadvantage of a whole life policy is the high outlay of premiums required in the early years.

The hybrid (whole-life/term combination). This relatively new product has some characteristics of both whole life and term insurance. The premiums are typically lower than a traditional whole life product but higher than a term policy. There is a buildup of cash value on these policies but at a lower rate than on the whole life policies. The percentage of whole life versus term insurance initially purchased will dictate the amount of the premium and the number of years you have to pay. Each year the dividend will automatically buy paid-up insurance to replace a portion of the term insurance; over a period of time the term is entirely replaced. In many cases the owner can vary the level of term insurance initially and then add money to the contract with very little or no commission taken out, thereby improving the overall performance of this policy.

Universal life. This relatively new type of insurance has as its primary advantage the aspect of flexibility. It is flexible with regard to the death benefit as well as the premiums paid and the ability to withdraw cash from the policy. Another possible advantage of a universal policy is that it can be more readily understood by the public. This contract is essentially a combination of an investment vehicle and term insurance. The insured makes premium payments to the contract which are credited with an interest rate on a monthly basis. Certain charges are taken out from the fund on a monthly basis. These include mortality costs and other administrative expenses.

A word of caution about universal life: The same feature that could be an advantage of this contract may become a disadvantage. The ability to vary the premium payments may put the insured in a position of having underfunded the contract in later years and seeing his coverage expire. This is particularly true when an agent or company has projected a high rate of return through the life of the policy, when in fact the economic environment dictates that a lower interest rate is actually credited to his account during many of these years. Besides being able to vary the face amount of coverage and the premium payments, the policy also allows for withdrawals of cash value from the policy without actually borrowing on the funds.

In order for you to determine what kind of insurance you need, it's important for you to step back and look at these insurance products from an overall perspective. This will mean asking the questions, How much do I need? (see the Insurance Needs Analysis Worksheet on pages 202–204), How long do I need it? and How much can I afford? Once you answer these questions, the appropriate product should become obvious.

For long-term needs, I recommend that you go with a strong mutual company with a good agent who will be around to service the product ten or twenty years down the road. The product type will depend on available cash, but the traditional whole life may be the best choice, although the other products mentioned certainly merit consideration.

Short-term needs can be met through term insurance, but here again I would recommend a higher-quality company over the lowest-cost term. This is because of convertibility, not insurability. (This is a key factor because a significant portion of term insurance is converted, and being with a quality company is a plus at the time of conversion.)

Insurance is a wise cornerstone of a complete financial plan, and it's necessary for peace of mind in the family unit. Although the marketplace can be confusing, thinking through the issues raised in this chapter should help you arrive at a sound decision. However, certain questions about insurance are common. I will address those before discussing the matter of estate planning.

Insurance Questions and Answers

What if I cannot afford the amount of insurance I need?
In this case you need to get all the insurance you can for the dollars available. A second step would be to make sure your family has a written plan

concerning the use of the insurance and alternatives for additional financial help (both spouses working, family help, where to get counsel, etc.).

Does a nonworking spouse need insurance?

If the insurance funds are limited, they belong on the breadwinner of the family. If the family is dependent on both spouses' income, then there may have to be some allocation to insurance for both. The least expensive way to do this is to include coverage for both as a part of the insurance coverage for the spouse earning the greatest income.

Do children need insurance?

Again, if insurance funds are limited, provide insurance for the breadwinner first. The purpose of insurance is provision. The children are not part of a family's provision.

There are four basic reasons for having insurance on a child:

1. To provide guaranteed insurability. This is a major point used in selling insurance for children. The idea implanted is that the child needs insurance in case he or she becomes disabled prior to becoming an adult and thus unable to qualify for insurance. The probability of this is very small.
2. To give them direction into a quality company at an early age.
3. For cash accumulation that can be used in purchasing other insurance policies at a later time.
4. Low rates at an early start.

Do not use insurance as a provision for education. Instead, let your budget and your priorities be your guide.

Is cash value or insurance with "savings" always a bad buy?

No, just usually more expensive. The economic aspect of insurance savings needs to be weighed carefully against other savings alternatives. Also, a long-term perspective may dictate a "permanent" insurance product.

When is cash-value insurance a good investment?

When it disciplines the insured to save money he might not otherwise have saved, or after a product has been held more than five years. (Older permanent policies may be good investments even though the death benefit may be somewhat smaller than with new products.)

When do I not need insurance?

When your investment assets reach the point that the income derived from them, plus other income that will not change in the event of death, will meet the provision you are responsible for. Until that time, insurance becomes an umbrella of protection to provide the needed resource in the event that you die before meeting your financial goals.

Retirement might be such a time. At retirement the income should be set. Its source might be Social Security, pension plans, annuities, or investments. If the spouse's needs are also met after the death of the provider, then there would not be a need for insurance to supply additional provision. There would also have to be no anticipated estate tax or liquidity needs.

At the other extreme, a young single person with no family or support responsibilities would have no need for insurance. An exception perhaps would be to have enough insurance so that burial costs or debt repayment would not present a burden to anyone.

Do insurance needs change?

They certainly do. Because of this, you should perform a periodic review of insurance with respect to your overall financial position and provision requirements. For example, when a man marries, he is responsible to provide for his wife. This may precipitate an insurance need. When children come along, the need for insurance may increase because of the need to assure that they are educated and then given an opportunity to make a living. Also, adequate capital is needed so the wife does not have to go to work and can spend time training the children. As children gain independence, the provision needs may decrease.

Other factors may prompt an insurance reevaluation:

- A significant rise in inflation.
- Increased income or lifestyle costs.
- Heavy personal or business debt obligations.
- A change in estate liquidity needs.
- Long-term flexibility.

Is insurance scriptural?

There is no mention in Scripture of insurance. The assumption would therefore be that it is not unscriptural. Scripture does emphasize trusting God. If insurance replaces trust in God, that is unscriptural. The key is to have a balanced attitude toward it.

If I foresee a long-term need for insurance, should I purchase whole-life insurance?

A long-term need means you have a need for insurance beyond age sixty-five. Most likely this would be for estate liquidity purposes or perhaps to provide flexibility in planning at that time in life. In this case, whole-life insurance, with its level premiums and lower costs (assuming it was purchased at a much younger age) would be the preferable product.

What about mortgage insurance?

Mortgage insurance is purchased for the exclusive purpose of paying off the debt on the home in the event of the death of the homeowner. It is actually a decreasing-term insurance, because, as the debt is decreased, the insurance company's liability is decreased. These policies are frequently more expensive than yearly renewable term products after the first several years. Most mortgage insurance is very expensive when reduced to the dollar cost per $1,000 of insurance base. This is especially the case if it is purchased through a mortgage company or bank. The alternative is to increase your existing life insurance to provide this coverage (if it is not already provided through a previous needs analysis) or to purchase a separate decreasing term-life insurance policy for this purpose and cancel it when the mortgage is paid.

Do I need credit life insurance on my loans?

As with mortgage insurance, credit insurance is very expensive. It is not recommended for that reason alone. In many cases, however, it is required by the lender as a condition of the loan. In that case, your only options are to find another lender, pay the price, save and pay cash, or forego the purchase.

Your Insurance Needs Analysis includes provision for debt payoff. Since debt varies, you may want to make a provision for an average amount of debt. Of course, the simplest way to deal with this area is to live debt-free as a part of your financial plan.

ESTATE PLANNING

A well thought-out estate plan will include not only a will, but also life insurance—correctly owned and with proper beneficiary designations, property deeded appropriately, survivors instructed in both written form and orally as to wishes and desires, proper and easily located records, advisors properly selected and instructed, and perhaps many other things. As can be seen, an estate plan is a very comprehensive plan for death, when planning is no longer possible. Therefore, it must be well-documented and totally complete. Unfortunately, it is estimated that 50 percent of Americans don't even have a will, let alone the other elements necessary for a complete and proper estate plan.

Reasons Given for Not Planning

"My estate is too small." An estate may be too small to have estate taxes due on it, but there is more to an estate plan than just the tax aspects. Appointing a guardian to care for any children is far too important a matter to be left to a total stranger. In addition, a relatively simple will can avoid many of the administrative costs associated with death.

When considering the size of an estate, many people forget that life insurance can add significantly to an estate size and may cause not only tax problems, but other types of problems as well.

One other reason for planning the estate rather than leaving it for the state court system to handle is that any particular personal effects you want to go to specific relatives or friends must be designated in a will. Otherwise, your intentions mean nothing, and the law of the land will determine who gets what.

"It's too expensive." Many people are "penny-wise and pound-foolish" and think that a will and other actions necessary for proper estate planning are too expensive. First of all, that thought may be an assumption and not a fact. My recommendation is to get an estimate or several estimates from those qualified to prepare the documents. On the other hand, probably no price is too great to pay for making it easier on friends and family who have never had to experience life without you.

"I don't have enough time." The underlying reason for this statement is probably a fear of death. Many people superstitiously believe that as long as they don't prepare a will, they won't die. Also, many just avoid talking about

death. It is a very uncomfortable topic of discussion for them. Again, with certainty, everyone will die and for the Christian to be superstitious about his or her death is to have a poor understanding of the promises God has made in the Bible.

"I'm not certain about what I want to do." Because estate planning can be a very complex and certainly unfamiliar topic, many do not know how to go about setting those objectives. This is a legitimate concern. However, God promises to provide us with the wisdom that we need (see James 1:5), and when we are planning for the future, we need God's wisdom for certain.

Also, no estate plan should be written in concrete. The design should always be flexible since our needs, desires, and circumstances change over time.

Estate Planning Objectives

Distribution of financial resources. There are only four alternatives available for the allocation of your financial resources: family and friends, charity, taxes, and expenses. You should plan this allocation after spending time with God so as to minimize the shrinkage from unnecessary expenses. The potential for conflict is great when it comes to predetermining priorities. My challenge to the people that I work with is to list these four alternatives and then to put either a percent or a dollar amount next to each one in order to quantify how they want their estate distributed. Generally speaking, if you can quantify where you want your estate to ultimately end up, then the estate plan can be drafted accordingly. The problem is that most people do not know or will not decide how they want their estate to be allocated.

Obviously, within the categories of family and friends and charity, there can be many alternatives.

Provide estate liquidity. Liquidity always provides flexibility. If an estate has any size at all, flexibility is needed to provide for the transition period immediately after one's death until assets can be transferred, retitled, and released. In addition, liquidity helps prevent the sale of nonliquid assets in perhaps an unfavorable economic environment when they would lose their true value. Liquidity is also needed to pay taxes, if any are due, and liquidity makes it easier to distribute an estate among several beneficiaries.

One of the most nonliquid assets that can typically have significant size is the value in a closely held business. By planning for the proper amount of liquidity, a closely held business can continue to function and provide the security needed for both the employees and owners. Insufficient liquidity can force the sale of a business at perhaps an inopportune time.

Provide for ease of management and administration of estate. Sometimes a wife is left after the death of her husband with no experience in managing assets. She undoubtedly would have the ability to do so with proper training, but suddenly she is overwhelmed with the responsibility for more money, from the life insurance and other assets, than she has ever managed. However, to select an executor or trustee other than a spouse may mean that control of the management and administration of the estate passes to a nonfamily member.

The person doing the estate planning must provide for the administration and management of the estate, taking into account the experience and ability of those appointed to this role. My advice is typically to name the spouse as executor and trustee because he or she can always hire any counsel that is needed to manage the estate's assets properly. When control is given to a corporate entity, such as a bank or a nonfamily member, then control literally passes out of the family's hands at the point of death, and that too often becomes a poor stewardship decision in retrospect. Story after story can be told of widows at the mercy of unsympathetic former business partners, bank trust officers, family friends, or even other family members.

I recommend that all parties affected by an estate plan review it together so their responsibilities can be clearly delineated by the one who is leaving the estate. While there is still opportunity, the individual should articulate his or her desires in front of all the family members and friends who are affected. Admittedly, this is something that is very, very rarely done—it never seems important until it is too late! In order to do this, I recommend a family conference. An explanation of the purpose of this conference and how to conduct one is included in the hardback edition of *Master Your Money*.

I always recommend that while he is alive a husband honor the absolute obligation to train his wife to manage whatever God has entrusted to the two of them. Otherwise, she has been effectively disinherited.

I remember visiting with a man who wanted me to help him plan his estate. He literally had several million dollars in cash that constituted his entire estate. He had no debts, a great marriage, and a desire to leave his estate ultimately to the Lord's work. As we were discussing the estate plan, he advised me that his wife had no idea how much they were worth. She trusted him implicitly with their financial situation and never questioned his decisions. However, when he described his intentions of giving away his entire estate, I asked him how his wife was going to feel when the will was read and she realized that she had had no part in determining where the millions were to go. They had several children, all of whom were at that time doing well spiritually and financially, but circumstances could change and his wife would have no opportunity to provide for any of the children or grandchildren under the proposed estate plan.

When I confronted him with his wife's potential feelings, he immediately saw the error in his thinking, went home, and shared his plans with his wife. Together they developed an estate plan that provided a bit more flexibility for her, but still accomplished the objectives he had for the ultimate distribution of the estate. Had the man not included his wife in determining the objectives for the estate, it could have been a very tragic story.

Provide for care of immediate family. When children are young, guardianship in the event of the death of both parents must be addressed. Also, the educational, physical, and mental or emotional needs of children may change with time. For example, a proper estate plan must be in place for a physically or mentally handicapped child. Older persons may plan to provide for the special needs of their grandchildren.

Providing for the care of the family also means that you have as an objective to maintain the lifestyle of the surviving spouse for some time period.

Provide for grown children. There is a fine line between provision and protection. We are to provide for our families, but not to the extent that they have no opportunity to trust God for work in their lives. Many children—and even young adults—have been ruined by overindulgent parents who left everything to them without considering the effect it could have in their children's lives.

It is a parent's responsibility, according to Proverbs 22:6, to "train up a child in the way he should go." That responsibility does not end when the child leaves home, and if the parents have failed in the training, then I suggest that they not compound that failure by leaving financial resources that protect the children from God's dealing with them in their adult lives.

I also believe that a parent should recognize differences in children— differences due to age, gender, temperament, demonstrated ability to handle money, spiritual commitment, spiritual maturity, known and unknown marriage partners, and children. It is a parent's and a grandparent's responsibility to entrust God's resources to children only if they have demonstrated the ability to handle those resources in a manner that would be pleasing to Him who is the owner of all.

If a parent entrusts God's resources to a slothful child, it is no different from giving those resources to any slothful stranger. Just because you have a child does not make the child the automatic beneficiary of your estate. The scriptural precedent is that the money should be left to those who have demonstrated sound stewardship. "Wisdom is good with an inheritance,/And profitable to those who see the sun./For wisdom is a defense as money is a defense,/But the excellence of knowledge is that wisdom gives life to those who have it" (Eccl. 7:11–12). According to the writer of Ecclesiastes, if we leave money to someone to whom we have not left wisdom it can be a devastating situation. I believe that more prayer, wisdom, and decisiveness are needed in meeting this objective of providing for grown children than any other estate-planning area. Obviously, great emotion and perhaps tradition are involved. Here again this is something that can and should be discussed in a family conference forum. Better to discuss unequal distributions to children while you are alive than to run the risk of bitterness toward you after you are dead.

Provide for charity. Unless you plan for charitable giving in your estate plan, it won't happen. Because any charitable gifts given at death are a deduction from the total estate for estate-tax purposes, all charitable giving at death reduces the estate taxes payable. The trade-off almost always becomes one between giving to family members and the government or giving to charity and is never an easy question to handle. My own belief is that the majority of charitable giving should be done while the income is being earned rather than delayed until death. After death, you have no more control over the property anyway, and it is not actually giving in the sense of giving up anything. Giving at death, however, is an opportunity to continue having an effect for Christ on earth while you are enjoying your new relationship with Him in heaven.

One means for your estate to continue to give to charity after your death is through a charitable trust, as described later in this chapter.

Provide testimony. My mother-in-law died recently. Along with her will was a note to her children that her greatest desire was for them to accept Jesus Christ as their personal Savior and to spend eternity with her.

She was sure of her relationship with Him. A will can provide a public record of your Christian testimony, not only for your children but also for anyone else who reads that document, including attorneys, judges, accountants, and perhaps grandchildren and great-grandchildren. Obviously, without a will, you do not have that written document of public testimony.

Provide for future planning flexibility. Because circumstances and desires change over time, very little of an estate plan should be written in concrete. In other words, irrevocable decisions need to be postponed, if possible, until death. The typical estate plan does not come into being until death. However, when an estate gets to be fairly sizeable, certain irrevocable decisions, such as property ownership, may have to be made. My recommendation is that all such decisions be made only when absolutely necessary and beneficial.

Estate-Planning Fundamentals

In order to understand some basic estate-planning techniques, it is essential to have a working knowledge of some basic estate terms.

Uniform federal estate and gift tax rates: the rate at which transfer of assets is taxed, whether the transfer occurs at death or as a gift during life, except for transfers to qualified charities (Unified Transfer Tax Rate Schedules shown on pages 216–217).

Unified Transfer Tax Rate Schedules

If the amount is:		Tentative tax is:		
Over	But not over	Tax	+ %	On excess over
0	$ 10,000	0	18	0
$ 10,000	20,000	$ 1,800	20	$ 10,000
20,000	40,000	3,800	22	20,000
40,000	60,000	8,200	24	40,000
60,000	80,000	13,000	26	60,000
80,000	100,000	18,200	28	80,000
100,000	150,000	23,800	30	100,000
150,000	250,000	38,800	32	150,000

250,000	500,000	70,800	34	250,000
500,000	750,000	155,800	37	500,000
750,000	1,000,000	248,300	39	750,000
1,000,000	1,250,000	345,800	41	1,000,000
1,250,000	1,500,000	448,300	43	1,250,000
1,500,000	2,000,000	555,800	45	1,500,000
2,000,000	2,500,000	780,800	49	2,000,000
2,500,000		1,025,800	*	2,500,000

*Varies based on year of death. Will be between 50–55%

Annual gift exclusion: the dollar amount of an asset or assets that can be transferred every year from any person to any other person or persons free from any gift transfer tax. The amount of the exclusion is $10,000. This exclusion provides for an attractive way to remove assets from one's estate with no tax erosion. For an illustration of how this can work in fairly large numbers, assume a couple has three children, all of whom are married and each of whom has two children. The three children plus three spouses plus six grandchildren makes a total of twelve family members. Because both the husband and the wife can each give $10,000 to each family member, potentially they can give $240,000 every year to their family—$10,000 from each parent to each child, spouse, and grandchild.

Marital gift exclusion: the amount of property that one spouse can transfer to the living spouse at his or her death without paying a transfer tax. The amount is unlimited. This can enable a person to avoid all estate tax at the death of the first spouse.

Unified credit: an estate and gift tax credit allowed by law to offset the tax due on any transfers of property which are taxed. The amount of the credit under current law is $192,800, which (referring to the tax-rate chart) will offset $600,000 of taxable property transferred. Both husband and wife will enjoy this credit so they could each transfer $600,000 of property to their children with no tax consequences, provided the assets are owned correctly.

Exemption equivalent: the value of the assets that can be offset by the unified credit. This value is $600,000, as stated previously.

Trust: A trust is simply a separate taxable entity that is set up during life or through a will to enable an individual to accomplish different desired planning objectives.

The will is the foundational cornerstone of an estate plan. It is a written, witnessed document that defines your final wishes and desires regarding many things, including property distribution. A person who dies with a will is called one who dies testate. A person who dies without a will dies intestate, and the laws of intestacy apply.

The laws of intestacy differ from state to state, but in general, if one dies intestate, that person gives the state government the right to determine:

- The control of the person's financial resources
- The distribution of those resources
- The choice of the executor
- The choice of a guardian for minor children
- The ability to waive fiduciary bonds
- The right to authorize a business continuation plan

On the other hand, a person who dies with a will retains the following:

- The control of the use of the person's assets
- The distribution of those assets
- The bequeathing of specific personal possessions to loved ones
- The choice of executor
- The choice of a guardian for minor children
- The right to waive fiduciary bonds (such bonds can be expensive)
- The right to set up various trusts to reduce estate taxes and probate costs

Types of Wills

There are basically three types of wills. The most common type, and the simplest, is the "I Love You" or Simple Will. This type of will simply states that the first spouse to die leaves everything to the surviving spouse. Under the Economic Recovery Tax Act (the new law passed in 1981), an unlimited marital deduction is allowed. This means that if all assets are left to your spouse, the first spouse to die would not pay any estate tax. This is a very attractive will for an estate that is under $600,000. However, since everything goes to the survivor, there could be a substantial tax at the survivor's death if the estate is over $600,000. To avoid this large potential tax problem at the death of the survivor, the second common type of will is used.

The second type of will is the A-B Trust Will. This type of will sets up one of two trusts. The objective is to keep a portion of the assets in the estate of the first spouse to die so as to utilize the "exemption equivalent." The exemption equivalent is the amount that any individual can have in his/her estate that is exempt from estate tax. (Under current law this amount is $600,000.)

For example, this type of will, instead of leaving everything to the spouse, will say something like "I leave everything to my spouse [outright or in trust] except the maximum amount I can keep in my estate and not be subject to estate tax [which, of course, could be as much as $600,000]. The amount kept in my estate will go into trust for the benefit of my spouse." (See The A-B Trust Will diagram on page 220.) If the first amount is left outright, we will have one trust. If it is left in trust, we end up with two trusts. (The legalese will be much different from the wording above, but in essence that is what happens.)

The terms of the trust that will hold the assets left in the decedent's estate (the first to die) are then written in such a way that the survivor has "virtual" ownership of the assets in the trust. In other words, he or she can get income and principal from the trust as needed. Another benefit of the trust is that it provides the surviving spouse with the assistance of a trustee in managing the assets.

Either the A-B Trust Will or the Simple Will meets the needs of most couples. However, in very complicated situations it may be important to go with the third type of will, which is call a "Pour-Over" Will. A Pour-Over Will simply leaves everything to a Revocable Trust that has already been set up. It is beyond the scope of this book to go into the details of this trust. Suffice it to say that one of the three types of wills we have described can and should be implemented, and you should seek professional advice to determine which fits your situation. The importance of having the wills is not only to plan your estate adequately, but—most importantly—to enable both spouses to achieve peace of mind.

Peace of mind is enhanced because of some very important appointments made in your wills. In your will, you will appoint an executor, a trustee, and a guardian if your children are minors. One of the problems with dying without a will is that the state already has a will for you. That will gives the state government the right to determine who is going to control your fi-

The A-B Trust Will

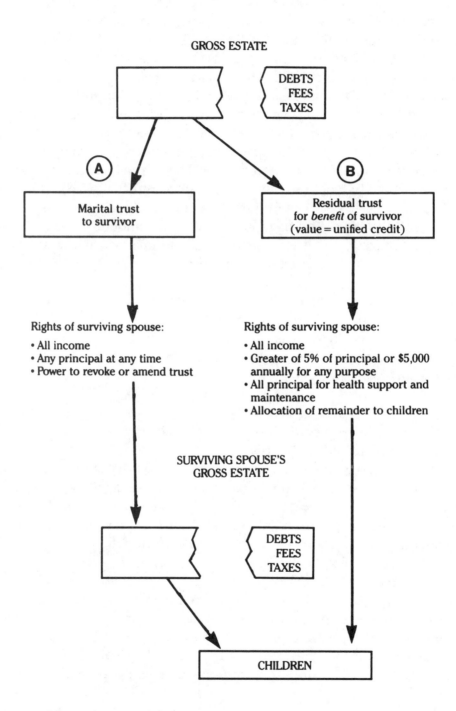

GROSS ESTATE

DEBTS
FEES
TAXES

Ⓐ

Ⓑ

Marital trust
to survivor

Residual trust
for *benefit* of survivor
(value = unified credit)

Rights of surviving spouse:

• All income
• Any principal at any time
• Power to revoke or amend trust

Rights of surviving spouse:

• All income
• Greater of 5% of principal or $5,000
  annually for any purpose
• All principal for health support and
  maintenance
• Allocation of remainder to children

SURVIVING SPOUSE'S
GROSS ESTATE

DEBTS
FEES
TAXES

CHILDREN

nancial resources, who is going to distribute those resources, and who is going to be the guardian for any minor children you may have. Therefore, the appointment of the executor, trustee, and guardian is an important reason to have a will.

The executor is responsible for assuming the property belonging to the estate, safeguarding and insuring the estate property during the period of estate settlement, and temporarily managing the estate while the estate is being settled. The person you designate will be involved in paying the estate taxes and expenses, accounting for the estate administration, and making distribution of the net estate to the heirs. The duties of the executor can be very time-consuming, frustrating, and complicated. For a surviving spouse, it can be overwhelming. In the will, a qualified individual or corporate trust company can be chosen to assist or fulfill all these duties.

The trustee is responsible for managing the estate left in trust in accordance with the terms of your will. Of course, if everything is left outright to your spouse, you do not need a trustee. The trustee could be a corporation, such as a bank, or an individual. I typically recommend having an individual trustee, since he or she is likely to be more responsive to the needs of the surviving spouse. This does not negate the fact that in many specific cases a bank trustee is preferred. (Professional counsel should be sought in making this trustee selection.) The executor and the trustee can be one and the same. Note: The trustee does not necessarily need to be knowledgeable in financial affairs, although that may help. Trustees usually seek outside expert financial advice from someone in the business (trust department, financial-planning firm). The key concerns in appointing both executor and trustee are, are they trustworthy, will they be sensitive to the needs of the family, and do they have integrity?

The guardian is someone you would trust to take over the care and upbringing of your minor children if something were to happen to each of you. Consideration should be given to the financial situation of the potential guardian; his or her health, age, and spiritual maturity; and the compatibility of that person's values with yours.

CONCLUDING OBSERVATIONS

There are many other technical aspects of estate planning that are beyond the scope of this book. Revocable living trusts, charitable remainder and charitable lead trusts, irrevocable life insurance trusts, as well as different methods of property ownership are all vehicles and techniques that could enhance an overall estate plan. The use of these will depend upon your goals, and the makeup and size of your estate and will require the input of a qualified professional.

Estate planning is an integral part of financial planning, but it is not financial planning in its entirety. Both financial planning and estate planning need to begin at an early age. They are dynamic in nature and to procrastinate in either area is poor stewardship.

Don't Miss the Miracle

Biblical Answers to the Questions of Giving

Americans are known as generous people. But exactly how generous are we?

- According to the IRS, 1.7 percent of adjusted gross income is the average charitable deduction taken on Form 1040, whereas the property tax and interest deduction (as indicators of the possessions that the bank and I own) is equal to 18 percent of adjusted gross income.
- Sam Erickson of the Christian Legal Society once did a personal study of average charitable giving. His conclusion was that all Americans gave, on the average, $.25 a day or $91 per year, and evangelical Christians gave an average of $1 a day or $365 per year.
- J. Robertson McQuilkin, president of Columbia Bible College, pointed out in a speech that if members of the Southern Baptist Convention alone would give an average of $100 per year to foreign missions, over $1.4 billion per year would be given. They are nowhere near that level now. If they were, the fulfillment of the

Great Commission could probably be financed rather easily in this generation by one denomination!

Several years ago a speaker at a missions conference in my church quoted the statistics that show that in the United States more money is spent on chewing gum and on dog food than is given to foreign missions. I cannot vouch for the accuracy of these numbers, but I do not doubt them. I do know the IRS reports that Americans, on the average, give less than 1.7 percent of their adjusted gross income for charitable contributions.

As a financial planner, my first paying client was a man who said his goal for the rest of his life was to retire just as soon as possible in order to work full time on the mission field. In addition, he wanted to maintain his present lifestyle and continue to give at the 15 percent level as he was then doing. He was a fifty-two-year-old physician with two children who had both already been educated. He had a net worth of around $350,000, and his income was approximately $85,000 per year. I asked him and his wife to share with me any dreams they might have for their lives. They both agreed that one of their desires was to give $1,000,000 to the Lord's work before they died. I thought to myself that this was obviously impossible with their income and net worth.

However, about sixty days later, after their financial plan was prepared, I called him.

"Doc, I hope you're sitting down, because I have some shocking news for you. First of all, how would you like to retire in five years and have approximately $1,000,000 in investments at that time?" I asked him.

He thought that sounded like a great idea! I then told him that, according to our projections, it was also possible for them to give away $1,000,000 during that same five-year time period. To say the least, he was shocked and frankly disbelieving.

I met with him and his wife to go over their plan and showed them that, in fact, they had a much higher net worth than they originally thought because of the escalation in value of some of the real estate they owned. By taking a long-range perspective on their planning, it was possible for them to begin giving away some of their assets while at the same time replacing them out of their current cash flow. Finally, I told them that all of this was possible for two reasons: first of all, because of their desire to give, and second, because they had lived and were continuing to live, a nonconsumptive lifestyle.

It has now been several years since we prepared their plan. Even though it did not work out exactly as projected, they have been fairly well able to accomplish the objectives they originally gave me . . . because God always has creative alternatives.

I have been able to share the same principles that I learned from this couple with others, and we have seen many clients make a commitment to giving substantial sums of money. From my observations I think there are three reasons why Christians who desire to give don't give more.

First of all, they don't know that they can give and still meet the other goals and objectives they have. They have never really gathered together an analysis of all their financial resources in order to know what obligations and opportunities they have. It is very difficult to be a good steward when you don't know what you have.

Second, they don't know how to give. They are not aware of all the various ways to give. In the doctor's case, one of the techniques that we used was to give away property that had appreciated in value, thereby avoiding the capital-gains tax on it. Furthermore, he still got a deduction for the full fair market value of the property. Through the use of this technique, he was able to reduce his taxes to a very low amount, which thus freed up cash to be invested in replacement of the property that had been given. It still cost him to do the giving, but it cost him less to give this way than if he had given cash.

The third and most important reason that people don't give is that they don't *plan* to give. It is the same issue that we have been dealing with throughout this book: We live a life of being a responder rather than a planner. In working with our clients, it has been my experience that, with planning, their giving, on an average, goes up to about four times what they were giving prior to planning. A very well-known and wealthy American told me one time, "Any man, and especially a businessman, has more uses for money than the money available. Therefore, unless he plans to give, he never will give." A person whose lifestyle is consumptive can never accumulate enough to be able to give substantial amounts of money away. Giving is never a cause of spiritual growth—it is rather a function of spiritual growth.

BIBLICAL ANSWERS TO THE QUESTIONS OF GIVING

There are three very relevant questions you should ask yourself as you plan to give:

1. When should I give?

2. Where should I give?
3. How much should I give?

As a result of reviewing guidelines and principles in the Bible, I believe there are six words that answer the questions of when to give, where to give, and how much to give:

1. When?
   • Preemptively
   • Periodically
2. Where?
   • Purposefully
3. How much?
   • Proportionately
   • Planned
   • Precommitted

When to give. Preemptive giving is clearly defined in Proverbs 3:9: "Honor the LORD with your possessions,/And with the firstfruits of all your increase." To me, this means that giving should have the first priority over all other uses of money, and therefore I give, preempting all other uses, until I have met that commitment.

"On the first day of the week let each one of you lay something aside, storing up as he may prosper, that there be no collections when I come" (1 Cor. 16:2). Not only should I give preemptively, but I should also give periodically. To take this scripture literally would be to say that, on each Sunday of the week, some amount should be put aside and saved for giving purposes. So the "when" question is answered—giving should be the first priority use of the income, and this giving should be done as it is received, that is, on a periodic basis.

Where to give. When answering the question Where should I give? we should make a purposeful decision to give where the Scripture says God's interest is. "For the administration of this service not only supplies the needs of the saints, but also is abounding through many thanksgivings to God" (2 Cor. 9:12).

God definitely commands us to meet the needs of the saints and to fulfill the Great Commission. Thus, our purposes in giving are to give for the needy, for evangelism, and for discipleship in our Judea, our Samaria, and the utmost parts of the earth (Acts 1:8). Giving must be taken very seriously and decided upon consciously in order to fulfill the commands of Scripture.

To help answer the question Where should I give? we can build a matrix. Down one side are the biblical admonitions to give to evangelism, discipleship, the poor, the widows, the orphans, and the needy. Across the top of the chart are the locations—Judea, Samaria, and the utmost parts of the earth, or in our contemporary situations, the city, the state, the United States, and the rest of the world.

As you review this giving plan, write in the giving that you are now doing. You will be able to see how well you are fulfilling the biblical admonitions in terms of places and needs. You then need to ask the question Am I giving all that I should be giving?

How much to give. How much to give in quantitative terms is not as important as our attitude toward giving. In 2 Corinthians 9:7 we read that our giving should be done "not grudgingly or of necessity: for God loves a cheerful giver." In 2 Corinthians 8:9, Paul gave us the example of Christ to suggest the right attitude toward giving: "For you know the grace of our Lord Jesus Christ, that though He was rich, yet for your sakes He became poor, that you through His poverty might become rich." So, the attitude of giving must be one of cheerfulness and grace. Freely we have received, freely we must give.

The question How much should I give? is not a simple matter. "For I bear witness that according to their ability, yes, and beyond their ability, they were freely willing, imploring us with much urgency that we would receive the gift and the fellowship of the ministering to the saints. And not only as we had hoped, but they first gave themselves to the Lord, and then to us by the will of God" (2 Cor. 8:3–5). Therefore, we are not limited in how much we give either by what we can see or according to our abilities.

Through consideration of the three P's we have mentioned we can come to a right answer of how much: we should give *proportionately* on a *planned* basis, and on a *precommitted* basis. Give an amount that is proportionate to the amount that God has prospered you. With planning, you should be able to give more than a proportionate amount, and you should precommit to giving some of the amount God provides on a totally unexpected basis.

Giving Plan

WHERE (Geographically)

WHAT (Activities)	MY CITY	MY STATE	MY COUNTRY	WORLD	HOW MUCH[1]
EVANGELISM	_____	_____	_____	_____	_____
DISCIPLESHIP	_____	_____	_____	_____	_____
POOR	_____	_____	_____	_____	_____
WIDOWS	_____	_____	_____	_____	_____
ORPHANS	_____	_____	_____	_____	_____
				TOTAL $ _____	

[1]How much:

Proportionately—should _____
Planned—could _____
Precommitted—would _____
TOTAL $ _____

When:

As received—Preemptively
—Periodically

WHAT DOES THIS MEAN TO ME?

These principles work themselves out in three levels of giving—the "should give" level, the "could give" level, and the "would give" level. The "should give" level includes our proportionate giving. Each Christian should give in proportion to the amount that he or she has received.

The "could give" level is the amount that I could give if I were willing to give up something else. It may mean that I give up a vacation, a savings account, a lifestyle desire, or something else. Giving at this level is the closest most American Christians can come to sacrificial giving as described in Luke 21:4: "For all these out of their abundance have put in offerings for God, but she out of her poverty put in all the livelihood that she had." Sacrificial giving is giving up something in order to give to the Lord. I recommend that after a financial plan is put together a family should regularly choose to give up something in order to give at the "could give" level. This level requires no faith, so it is not a faith pledge. There is no faith required because you can see the amount, and faith, by definition, requires trusting in the unseen.

The third level of giving more clearly approximates faith giving, and I call it the precommitted giving or the "would give" level. We commit ourselves to giving if God provides a certain amount supernaturally. God can do this only if there is a financial plan in place that allows us to see His providing an additional cash-flow margin through either additional income or decreased expense. Unless we are precommitted to give the additional surplus, we will not give it.

In summary, how much we give is dependent upon our giving at three levels: I should give an amount proportionate to my income; I could give an additional amount by giving up something; and I would give more if God increased my cash-flow margin. The how much is not dependent upon a set formula, and it gives us the opportunity to see God at work in our financial lives.

Many times I am asked whether one should give now or should build an investment base in order to be able to give later. In our earlier illustrations, we saw that $10,000 compounding at 25 percent over forty years grows to $75,231,000. Wouldn't a person do better to find an investment at 25 percent to compound it and then give the $75,231,000 rather than the mere $10,000?

The way I answer this question is with another question, Is God limited to 25 percent compounding? Even though there is no biblical interest rate stated, the Bible does point out in many places that he who sows sparingly shall also reap sparingly, and that God causes fruit to grow at 30-fold, 60-fold and 100-fold rates. In percentage terms, 30-fold is 3,000 percent; 60-fold is 6,000 percent; and 100-fold is 10,000 percent. I don't believe it is wrong to assume that God's rate of compounding is 3,000 percent, 6,000 percent, 10,000 percent, and even greater.

Then I would ask the question Is an investment of $10,000, compounding at 25 percent, comparable to giving the amount of $10,000, compounding at 10,000 percent, for all eternity? That is the real comparison.

> Do not lay up for yourselves treasures on earth, where moth and rust destroy and where thieves break in and steal; but lay up for yourselves treasures in heaven, where neither moth nor rust destroys and where thieves do not break in and steal. For where your treasure is, there your heart will be also.
>
> The lamp of the body is the eye. If therefore your eye is good, your whole body will be full of light. But if your eye is bad, your whole body will be full of darkness. If therefore the light that is in you is darkness, how great is that darkness!
>
> No one can serve two masters; for either he will hate the one and love the other, or else he will be loyal to the one and despise the other. You cannot serve God and mammon.
>
> —Matthew 6:19–24

In the Sermon on the Mount, Jesus makes it clear that our treasure will either be on earth ($75,231,000) or in heaven ($10,000 x 10,000 percent x eternity). Without question, the eternal perspective on giving makes the temporal perspective of no consequence.

As someone once said to me, "Do your giving while you're living so you're knowing where it's going." And the martyred missionary Jim Elliott said, "He is no fool who gives up what he cannot keep in order to gain what he cannot lose." Whether to give now or later is really a silly question when you put it into the perspective of the Almighty.

God is perfectly able to handle your investment of His resources in His kingdom and to cause it to grow and to compound at the greatest rate. He does not need your expertise nor skill to cause an investment to grow in order for you to be able to give more later.

The Faith Giving Pledge on page 235 gives you an opportunity to make a faith giving pledge for the coming year. It breaks the faith giving pledge down to the three levels of giving—what you should give, what you could give, and what you would give. You cannot complete this pledge until:

1. You have summarized your financial situation and determined what amount of proportionate giving you are going to do.
2. You know what amount of sacrificial giving you are going to do by giving up something.
3. You know what your cash flow margin is—that which you would give if God caused it to be more than you anticipated.

My challenge for you is to prayerfully make the pledge and then watch what God does to cause it to become a reality!

DON'T MISS THE MIRACLE

I have often wondered what it is going to be like to stand before the Lord and have Him evaluate my works. I wonder whether I will hear Him say, "Well done, good and faithful servant; you were faithful over a few things, I will make you ruler over many things. Enter into the joy of your lord" (Matt. 25:21). Or, on the other hand, will I watch as most of the works that I have accomplished are consumed by fire? My greatest fear is that I may fervently work at the wrong task rather than faithfully complete God's work for me.

Mark 6 is a passage on which I often reflect.

> The apostles gathered to Jesus and told Him all things, both what they had done and what they had taught. And He said to them, "Come aside by yourselves to a deserted place and rest a while." For there were many coming and going, and they did not even have time to eat.
>
> So they departed to a deserted place in the boat by themselves. But the multitudes saw them departing, and many knew Him and ran there on foot from all the cities.
>
> They arrived before them and came together to Him. And Jesus, when He came out, saw a great multitude and was moved with compassion for them, because they were like sheep not having a shepherd. So He began to teach them many things.
>
> When the day was now far spent, His disciples came to Him

and said, "This is a deserted place, and already the hour is late. Send them away, that they may go into the surrounding country and villages and buy themselves bread; for they have nothing to eat."

But He answered and said to them, "You give them something to eat."

And they said to Him, "Shall we go and buy two hundred denarii worth of bread and give them something to eat?"

But He said to them, "How many loaves do you have? Go and see."

And when they found out they said, "Five, and two fish."

Then He commanded them to make them all sit down in groups on the green grass. So they sat down in ranks, in hundreds and in fifties. And when He had taken the five loaves and the two fish, He looked up to heaven, blessed and broke the loaves, and gave them to His disciples to set before them; and the two fish He divided among them all. So they all ate and were filled.

And they took up twelve baskets full of fragments and of the fish. Now those who had eaten the loaves were about five thousand men.

—Mark 6:30–44

CONCLUSIONS

Many conclusions that are applicable to financial planning can be drawn from this passage because financial planning is, in reality, the working out of the priorities of life. Let's examine the principles I have gleaned from this passage.

Principle 1. Jesus said, "Come aside by yourselves to a deserted place and rest a while" (Mark 6:31). The first step to financial planning is to be alone with Jesus and listen to what He has to say. It is not the development of a plan, it is not getting advice, but it is spending time alone with Him.

Unless you hear God's voice, you cannot take a second step. Jesus recognized this principle, and it is obvious in His life because He spent much time alone with God prior to making any major decision. Can we do less?

Principle 2. "Jesus, when He came out, saw a great multitude and was moved with compassion for them, because they were like sheep not having a shepherd. So He began to teach them many things" (Mark 6:34). A second principle is that our plan should not be our god. Jesus had a plan to go with His disciples to a quiet place; however, when He saw the needs, He had compassion on the people and was responsive to God's direction in His life at that point. To be totally committed to a plan is to make a serious mistake. God works in our lives through many circumstances and to ignore them because a plan is in place is to run the risk of missing God's will.

Principle 3. "His disciples came to Him and said, "This is a deserted place, and already the hour is late. Send them away, that they may go into the surrounding country and villages and buy themselves bread" (Mark 6:35–36). I have often asked myself. What's wrong with this advice? The answer is, nothing—except that it was wrong. It was very practical and logical, but it was not in accordance with what Jesus intended at that point. Two guidelines come from this passage: First of all, don't ever thwart God because of a merely practical consideration. God wants to do things in His way, in His time. Practicality does not always coincide with faith. It is not wrong in itself; it is just wrong in light of what God wants to accomplish.

The second principle that comes out of this advice is that worldly advice can be logical, but it is not necessarily right. Many Christians fall into the trap of listening to non-Christian counselors and expect the non-Christian counselors to give them godly advice. The advice may sound good and may even be good, but unless it is advice that comes from God, it is wrong.

Principle 4. The disciples argued a bit with Jesus regarding His plan, but Jesus did not argue back. Finally He directed them to have all the people sit down on the grass. This was very illogical because, at that point, they did not have the food to feed them. The principle that comes out of this is that we must be obedient. No questions asked. If God says to do it, I do it. If God says to give, I give. If God says to pay off debt—I do it. If God says to accumulate to pay my taxes, I do so. If God says to increase or decrease my lifestyle, I do so. The issue is *obedience*.

Principle 5. In verse 40, when the disciples had the people sit down on the grass, there were three elements present that are always present in a faith plan. First of all, they obviously could not see how the people were going to be fed. Oftentimes, in a financial plan, we may not see how our goal is going to be accomplished either. Second, there were without question inadequate resources to accomplish the disciples' objective, and that also may be characteristic of our financial plan—that we have inadequate resources. Third, the disciples did not know what the next step to fulfill God's plan was going to be. Thus, a faith plan for us may require action without our full understanding. I think of Noah's building an ark for one hundred years, not fully understanding what God was going to do, or Abraham's leaving Ur, not knowing what God was going to do.

Principle 6. Verses 42–43 say, "They all ate and were filled. And they took up twelve baskets full of fragments and of the fish." The results of operating according to a faith plan are that the goal will be reached, God will be glorified, and growth will occur. In the case of the five thousand, the goal was reached, the Lord received the glory, and the disciples *should* have experienced growth in their faith.

However, if you read on in the passage, you come down to verses 51–52, "Then He went up into the boat to them, and the wind ceased. And they were greatly amazed in themselves beyond measure, and marveled. For they had not understood about the loaves, because their heart was hardened." What a tragedy! Just a few hours earlier they had seen an unbelievable miracle. As a matter of fact, they had participated in the miracle by handing out the bread and fish, and then gathering up the twelve baskets of leftovers. However, the Scripture says, "They were greatly amazed in themselves beyond measure, and marveled. For they had not understood about the loaves, because their heart was hardened."

The challenge is, don't plan God out of your finances. Don't have a closed mind. *Don't miss the miracle.* I hope that much has been given to you in this book that is practical and useful; but don't miss the miracle of what God wants to do in your life by saying, "It is not appropriate or applicable in my situation, for surely God could not want to do that for me."

God merely wants you to take the first step, then the second step, then the third step, so that when you stand before Him, you will finally understand that whatever has been accomplished has been accomplished by Him. Because of your faithfulness with regard to what He has given you, you will hear Him say, "Well done, good and faithful servant; you were faithful over a few things, I will make you ruler over many things. Enter into the joy of your lord" (Matt. 25:21).

Faith Giving Pledge

Recognizing that God wants us to be good stewards of His resources and to use them for His purposes, we make the following giving pledge for the coming year

Amount

What we should give: $_____

What we could give by making a sacrifice in the
following area: $_____

_____

What we will give if God blesses us with additional
cash-flow margin: $_____

We will give: $_____

_____
Name

_____
Name

PART THREE

A Forward Look

FINANCIAL PLANNING
IN AN UNCERTAIN ECONOMY

The forty-five years following World War II have seen an incredible growth in our affluence as a nation. No people as a whole, *ever,* have possessed the material resources that we do. We are truly a blessed people, and yet there are some significant cracks in our economic structure.

Our national debt (the amount of money owed by our government) recently went over three trillion dollars, or approximately $15,000 for every man, woman, and child in our country. If we wanted to pay off this debt, we would first of all have to stop going into debt; and then if we started a repayment plan of one million dollars per day, it would still take over 3,000 years to pay back the debt. We have mortgaged not only our children's future, but obligated countless future generations. Someone must pay this debt through a literal repayment (future taxes), a deceitful repayment (future inflation), or cancellation (political upheaval). There are no other alternatives. The debt will not merely disappear.

I could go on and on about how serious our economic problems are. For example, what happens to our banking system if Third World countries refuse to repay their debts to American banks? Who is going to pay for the savings and loan losses? What happens to our economy if Japan's economy fails? The fact of the matter is, the problems are serious, and there is absolutely nothing you or I, as individuals, can do to solve them.

More than two hundred years ago, while the original thirteen colonies were still part of Great Britain, Professor Alexander Tyler wrote of the Athenian republic, which had fallen two thousand years earlier:

> A democracy cannot exist as a permanent form of government. It can only exist until the voters discover that they can vote themselves a largesse from the [public] treasury. From that moment on, the majority will always vote for the candidates promising the most benefits from the public treasury, with the result that a democracy always collapses over loose fiscal policy and is always followed by a dictatorship.

The average age of the world's greatest civilizations has been 200 years. These nations have progressed through this sequence: from *bondage* to *spiritual faith;* from *spiritual faith* to *great courage;* from *great courage* to *abundance;* from *abundance* to *selfishness;* from *selfishness* to *complacency;* from *complacency* to *apathy;* from *apathy* to *dependency;* from *dependency* back again into *bondage.*

There is no question that the United States is at least at the abundance level in the sequence outlined by Professor Tyler. In my opinion we are leaving the selfishness level and approaching complacency.

Before you wring your hands in despair, let me give you a question to ponder. Do you think God is worried? Is He wringing His hands in despair, wondering how it is all going to turn out? Of course not! Inflation, deflation, monetary collapse, and political upheavals are nothing new to Him; and His message is just as relevant today as it was 2,000 years ago.

The context, then, of personal money management is that God is still in control and under His control there are only four possible economic situations: (1) inflation, (2) deflation, (3) monetary collapse, or (4) political upheaval. Although I am neither an economist nor a prophet and I do not know what is going to happen, I can plan for possible eventualities, and base my planning on biblical principles.

My opinion about what is going to happen is based on the nature of all people to be selfish. A selfish person placed in an environment of almost unlimited opportunity to be selfish (our country, or any shopping mall) will always react with greed. If greed can be funded on an unlimited basis (consumer debt), it will produce inflation. Prices will rise because, with the unlimited opportunity for debt, only the repayment is relevant. Inflation, over time, will always produce a monetary collapse because the currency has become worthless.

Do I believe this will really occur? Yes, I do believe it will happen; but God is sovereign and can change the course of our history in any way He wants.

In any case, financial planning must take place under the sovereignty of God, recognizing His omnipotence, wisdom, purposes, and plans. Because there are only four economic possibilities, I must plan for all four. The steps you have taken in working through the *Master Your Money* financial planning process are sound financially, no matter what takes place in our economy.

I believe that God is more interested in each of us individually than He is in any failure or success of our economic system. I do not believe that the Bible sets forth any one economic system. God is interested in how I glorify Him wherever I live, whether under capitalism, communism, socialism, or any other system.

God has called each of us, as Christians, to a unique role in our uncertain economy.

Glossary

After-Tax Return—The yield of an investment after taxes have been taken out.

Annuity—An individual pays an insurance company a specified capital sum in exchange for a promise that the insurer will, at some time in the future, begin to make a series of periodic payments to the individual for as long as he/she lives or for some other specified period of time.

Appreciation—An increase in fair market value.

Assets—Everything a person owns, including cash, investments, accounts receivable, real property, autos, etc.

Balance Sheet—A condensed financial statement showing the amount and nature of an individual's assets and liabilities at a given time. A "snapshot" of what a person owns and what he owes. Sometimes referred to as net worth statement.

Basis—The price paid for an asset. Used to figure capital gains tax.

Beneficiary—One who is designated to receive a benefit, for example, the person who would receive the proceeds of a life insurance settlement.

Bid and Asked—The "bid" is the highest price anyone is willing to pay for a security at a given time; the "asked" is the lowest price anyone will take at that time. Stocks are usually purchased at "bid" and sold at "asked."

Bond—A promise of a corporation, municipality, government, church, etc., to pay interest at a stated rate and repay face value of the bond (which is actually a loan from you to the corporation, etc.) at a specified maturity date.

Budget—A plan or guideline for spending.

Capital Gain—Profit or loss from the sale of a capital asset such as real estate, stock, commercial property, land, equipment, etc. Any capital asset held at least one year is classified as long-term and receives favorable income tax treatment. (Only 40 percent of profit is taxed.)

Capital Needs—In personal financial planning, the amount of capital (assets or cash) needed in a lump sum to enable one to meet income needs and expenses should death or disability occur.

Cash Flow—The process of money coming in from various sources (income) and being spent on various uses (expenses). A cash-flow statement is a look at both the income and the expenses over any period of time, but is usually for at least a month and/or for a year.

Cash Surrender Value—The actual value of your life insurance policy. It is the amount of cash you would receive if you voluntarily terminate your policy before it matures. It is also the amount that can be borrowed from your policy while still keeping the policy in force. This value can be found in the policy contract. It may be more than the contract value, as it can be increased by dividends and interest on dividends which are left to accumulate (dividend deposits).

Common Stock—Securities that represent an ownership interest in a corporation. Generally have dividend and appreciation potential.

Cost Per Thousand—Refers to the cost of each thousand dollars of life insurance protection.

Current Assets—Those assets that can easily be converted into cash or sold in a short period of time. Example: stocks, certificates of deposit, cash value of life insurance, money market funds, etc. Also known as liquid assets.

Debt—A sum owed to someone else, either a financial or personal obligation; a state of owing.

Diversification—Spreading money among different types of investments.

Dividends—The payment designated by a corporation to be distributed pro-rata among outstanding shares of stock. Corporations usually declare dividends from their profits, and the amount is in relation to the amount of the profit.

Dividend Election—The method you choose to receive your dividends. Most commonly refers to life insurance. You may elect dividends to be paid in cash, to reduce premiums, to buy paid-up additions, or to accumulate at interest.

Dollar Cost Averaging—A method of purchasing securities at regular intervals with a fixed amount of dollars, regardless of the prevailing prices of the securities. Payments buy more shares when the price is low and fewer shares when it rises. Because of the fluctuations of the market, this method enables an investor who consistently buys in both good and bad times to be able to improve his potential for a gain when he sells. It is an effective method for a single investor to strategically invest his money.

Effective Rate—The amount of each dollar earned which goes to pay taxes. The ratio of total taxes paid to gross income.

Face Value—The amount the insurance company promises to pay at death of insured.

Fiduciary—One who acts for another in financial matters.

Fixed—Refers to an asset principal which cannot grow in value. You will never get back more or less than you invested. Example: certificates of deposit, cash value, bonds, etc. These assets are fixed yield in nature.

Individual Retirement Account (IRA)—A retirement provision established by law which allows an individual to deduct from his income a certain amount set aside for future retirement. Under the Economic Recovery Tax Act of 1981, all workers are eligible for an IRA, and may contribute up to $4,000/year in the case of a married couple with both spouses working.

Inflation—An increase in the volume of money and credit relative to available goods resulting in a substantial and continuing rise in the general price level.

Inflationary Spiral—A continuous rise in prices that is sustained by the interaction of usage increases and cost increases.

Investment—The use of money for the purpose of making more money: to gain income, increase capital, save taxes, or a combination of the three.

Keogh or Self-employed Retirement Plan—Similar to an IRA, but designed for the self-employed individual. The Keogh permits the setting aside of a specified part of current earnings for use as a retirement fund in the future. The Economic Recovery Tax Act of 1981 also contained significant changes and provisions for Keogh plans. Beginning in 1982 a self-employed individual may contribute the lesser of 15 percent of his income or $15,000.

Leverage—The use of a small amount of equity or assets to control or purchase an asset worth substantially more. The value to the investor is that you receive appreciation on the total worth of the asset, not just your equity. Although leveraging increases your earnings potential, one is "at risk" for the amount leveraged (the loan). Example: If you put $10,000 down and borrow $70,000 to buy an $80,000 home, you have leveraged.

Liabilities—All the claims against you. Obligations you owe. Some may be current (owed within the year), such as credit card loans; others may be long term, such as a home mortgage.

Liquidity (Liquid)—The state of assets readily converted to cash at their current fair market value. (Will not lose value upon sale as a result of a lack of a ready market.)

Long-Term Assets (Nonliquid)—Those assets which cannot easily be converted to cash or sold or consumed in a short period of time. Example: home, real estate, land assets, etc.

Margin—The cash sources less the cash uses. The amount you have left to spend as you desire after all living expenses, mandatory commitments, and taxes are met.

Marginal Rate—The tax bracket percentage from which your income tax is calculated. For example, in the case of a person in the 28 percent tax bracket, twenty-eight cents of each additional dollar earned would go to the government in taxes.

Marital Deduction—In calculating estate tax, a deduction allowed by law against the estate of the first spouse to die. The amount of the qualifying property or deduction under the new Economic Recovery Tax Act of 1981 is the entire estate of the first to die.

Minimum Deposit—When the cash-value increases in the insurance policy are used to pay the premiums of the policy.

Money Market Fund—A mutual fund that invests in money-market instruments such as treasury bills, U.S. Government agency issues, commercial bank certificates of deposit, commercial paper, etc. The interest rate on a money market fund fluctuates with the prime interest rate.

Mortgage—Usually refers to the balance of the loan on a home. The amount of money borrowed to purchase a home.

Nonliquid—Investments not easily converted to cash at their current fair market value.

Preferred Stock—Similar to common stock. Generally less dividend and appreciation potential but receives a higher priority or preference over common stock in dividend payments or in the event of liquidation.

Premium—The payment an insurance policy holder agrees to make for coverage.

Present Value—The value of a sum of money to be received in the future in today's dollars, taking into account either interest rates, inflation, or both. (Example: $10,000 received in 1985 has a present value of $6,830.)

Prime Rate—The interest rate charged by large U.S. money center commercial banks to their best business borrowers.

Principal—A person's capital or money. Used for investments. Sometimes referred to as equity when talking about a house.

Prospectus—A circular that describes securities or investments being offered for sale to the public.

Purchasing Power—The ability of a dollar to buy a product or service. As prices increase, purchasing power decreases. Today's dollar will not buy as much today as it would in 1970.

Unified Credit—A credit, established by law, applied to tentative Federal Estate Taxes owed upon death of an individual.

Variable—Refers to assets which have the potential to grow; primarily concerned with appreciation. Examples: stocks, real estate, etc. These may be sold for more or less than you invested.

Will—The directions of a testator (the male or female who makes the will) regarding the final disposition of his or her estate.

Withholding—Refers to the amount of tax withheld from a paycheck.

Withholding Allowances—Used by an employer to calculate the amount withheld monthly from your check for federal and state taxes.

Yield—Dividends or interest paid by a company expressed as a percentage of current selling price.

About the Author

Ron received his Master of Business Administration degree from Indiana University, then served for three years in the management group of Peat, Marwick, Mitchell & Co. in New York City, Dallas, and San Francisco.

In 1970, he founded Blue & Co. in Indianapolis, which is now one of the 50 largest CPA firms in the United States.

In 1977, he left Blue & Co. to become Administrative Vice President of Leadership Dynamics International, where he was involved in developing and teaching biblically-based leadership and management seminars to Christians throughout the United States and Africa.

Convinced that Christians would better handle their personal finances if they were counseled objectively with the highest technical expertise and from a biblical perspective, he founded Ronald Blue & Co. in 1979. Ronald Blue & Co. is a fee-only professional firm providing services to individuals in the areas of tax planning, charitable gifting, investment planning, estate planning, family budgeting, and more.

Serving over 1000 clients nationwide, Ronald Blue & Co. employs a staff of over 60 in its headquarters in Atlanta and branch offices in Indianapolis, Orlando, Phoenix, and Holland, MI.

Ron is the author of the best-selling book *Master Your Money, Raising Money-Smart Kids,* co-authored with his wife Judy, *The Debt Squeeze,* and his latest release, also co-authored with Judy, *A Woman's Guide to Financial Peace of Mind.*

Ron is featured in a six-part video series, *Master Your Money,* which is a curriculum that brings together biblical principles and sound financial concepts. *The Master Your Money* video has been used in over 4,000 churches across the country. He has also appeared on numerous radio and television shows including Focus on the Family, The 700 Club, and Prime Time America. He is a regular columnist for *Moody Monthly, Physicians,* and *Marriage Partnership* magazines.

Ron, Judy, and their five children live in Atlanta.